biscuits, baking & cakes

essential recipes

Publisher's Note:
Raw or semi-cooked eggs should not be consumed by babies, toddlers, pregnant women,
the elderly or those suffering from recurring illness.

Publisher and Creative Director: Nick Wells
Project Editor: Cat Emslie
Photographers: Paul Forrester, Colin Bowling and Stephen Brayne
Home Economists & Stylists: Jaqueline Bellefontaine, Mandy Phipps,
Vicki Smallwood and Penny Stephens
Art Director: Mike Spender
Layout Design: Dave Jones
Digital Design and Production: Chris Herbert
Editorial Assistant: Chelsea Edwards
Proofreader: Dawn Laker

12 11

5 7 9 10 8 6

This edition first published 2008 by
FLAME TREE PUBLISHING
Crabtree Hall, Crabtree Lane
Fulham, London SW6 6TY
United Kingdom

www.flametreepublishing.com

Flame Tree is part of the Foundry Creative Media Co. Ltd
© 2008 The Foundry Creative Media Co. Ltd

ISBN 978-0-85775-001-3

A CIP Record for this book is available from the British Library upon request

Printed in China

biscuits, baking
& cakes

essential recipes

General Editor: Gina Steer

**FLAME TREE
PUBLISHING**

Contents

Everyday Cakes 112

Biscuits, Cookies, Brownies & Traybakes 152

Celebration Cakes, Cream Cakes & Gateaux 190

Equipment

Cooking equipment not only assists in the kitchen, but can make all the difference between success and failure. Take the humble cake tin: although a very basic piece of cooking equipment, it plays an essential role in baking. A tin that is too large will spread the mixture too thinly and the result will be a flat, limp-looking cake. On the other hand, cramming the mixture into a tin which is too small will result in the mixture rising up and out of the tin. A few, well-picked, high quality utensils and pieces of equipment will be frequently used and will therefore be a much wiser buy than cheaper gadgets.

Baking Equipment

Follow the manufacturer's instructions when first using a cake tin and ensure that it is thoroughly washed and dried after use. Perhaps the most useful of tins are sandwich cake tins, ideal for classics such as Victoria sponge, genoese and coffee and walnut cake. You will need two tins and they are normally 18 cm/7 inches or 20.5 cm/8 inches in diameter, about 5–7.5cm/2–3 inches deep, and are often non-stick.

With deep cake tins, it is personal choice whether you buy round or square tins, and they vary in size from 12.5–35.5 cm/5–14 inches with a depth of between 12.5–15 cm/5–6 inches. A deep cake tin, for everyday fruit or Madeira cake is a must – a useful size is 20.5 cm/8 inches. Loaf tins are used for bread, fruit or tea bread and terrines and normally come in two sizes, 450 g/1 lb and 900 g/2 lb.

Good baking sheets are a must. Dishes that are too hot to handle such as apple pies should be placed directly on to a baking tray. Meringues and biscuits are also cooked on a baking tray. Do not confuse these with Swiss roll tins which have sides all around: a sheet only has one raised side.

Square or oblong shallow baking tins are also very useful for making tray bakes, brownies, flapjacks and shortbread. Patty tins are ideal for making small buns, jam tarts or mince pies, while individual Yorkshire pudding tins and muffin tins

are also useful. They are available in a variety of sizes. There are plenty of other tins to choose from, from themed and shaped, to spring-form tins where the sides release after cooking allowing the cake to be removed easily. Three to four different sizes of mixing bowls are also very useful.

Another piece of equipment worth having is a wire cooling rack. It is essential when baking to allow biscuits and cakes to cool after being removed from their tins.

A selection of different-sized roasting tins are also a worthwhile investment as they can double up as a bain-marie, or for cooking larger quantities of cakes such as gingerbread. Ramekin dishes and small pudding basins can be used for a variety of different recipes, as can small tartlet tins and dariole moulds.

Perhaps the rolling pin is one of the most important baking implements. Ideally it should be long and thin, heavy enough to roll the pastry out easily but not too heavy that it is uncomfortable to use. Pastry needs to be rolled out on a flat surface, and although a lightly floured flat surface will do, a marble slab will keep the pastry cool and ensure that the fats do not melt while being rolled. This helps to keep the pastry light, crisp and flaky rather than heavy and stodgy.

Other useful basic pastry implements are tools such as a pastry brush (which can be used to wet pastry or brush on a glaze), a pastry wheel for cutting and a sieve to remove impurities and also to sift air into the flour, encouraging the pastry or mixture to be lighter in texture.

Basic mixing cutlery is also essential, such as a wooden spoon (for mixing and creaming), a spatula (for transferring the mixture from the mixing bowl to the baking tins and spreading the mixture once it is in the tins) and a palette knife (to ease cakes and breads out of their tins before placing them on the wire racks to cool). Measuring spoons and cups are essential for accurate measuring of both dry and wet ingredients.

Electrical Equipment

Nowadays help from time-saving gadgets and electrical equipment make baking far more easy and quick. Equipment can be used for creaming, mixing, beating, whisking, kneading, grating and chopping. There is a wide choice available from the most basic to the very sophisticated.

Food Processors

W hen choosing a machine, you must first decide what you need it to do. If you are a novice, it may be a waste to start with a machine that offers a wide range of implements and functions. This can be off-putting and result in not using the machine to its full capabilities.

In general, while styling and product design play a role in the price, the more you pay, the larger the machine will be, with a bigger bowl capacity and many more gadgets attached. However, just what basic features should you ensure your machine has before buying it? When buying a food processor look for measurements on the side of the processor bowl and machines with a removable feed tube which allows food or liquid to be added while the motor is still running. Look out for machines that have the facility to increase the capacity of the bowl (ideal when making soup) and have a pulse button for controlled chopping.

For many, storage is also an issue, so reversible discs and flex storage, or on more advanced models, a blade storage compartment or box, can be advantageous.

It is also worth thinking about machines that offer optional extras that can be bought as your requirements change. For instance, mini chopping bowls are available for those wanting to chop small quantities of food. If time is an issue, dishwasher-friendly attachments may be vital.

Blenders

Blenders often come as attachments to food processors and are generally used for liquidising and puréeing. There are two main types. The first is known as a goblet blender. The blades are at the bottom of the goblet with measurements up the sides. The second is portable. It is hand-held and should be placed in a bowl to blend.

Food Mixers

These are ideally suited to mixing cakes and kneading dough, and are either table-top or hand-held. The table-top mixers are freestanding and are capable of dealing with fairly large quantities. They are robust and capable of easily dealing with kneading and heavy cake mixing as well as whipping cream, whisking egg whites or making one-stage cakes. Hand-held mixers are smaller and often come with their own bowl and stand from which they can be lifted off and used as hand-held devices. They have a motorised head with detachable whisks. These mixers are particularly versatile as any suitable mixing bowl can be used.

Basic Techniques

There is no mystery to successful baking, it really is easy providing you follow a few simple rules. First, read the recipe right through before commencing. Until you are confident with a recipe do not try any short cuts, or you may find that you have left out a vital step.

Pastry Making

Pastry needs to be kept as cool as possible throughout. Cool hands help. Use cold or iced water, but not too much as pastry does not need to be wet. Make sure that your fat is not runny or melted but firm (this is why block fat is the best). Avoid using too much flour when rolling as this alters the proportions, and also avoid handling the dough too much. Roll in one direction as this ensures that the pastry does not shrink. Allow pastry to rest after rolling, preferably in the refrigerator. If your pastry is still not as good as you would like it to be, then make it in a processor instead.

Lining a Flan Case

It is important to choose the right tin to bake with. You will often find that a loose-bottomed metal flan case is the best option as it conducts heat more efficiently and evenly than a ceramic dish. It also has the added advantage of a removable base, which makes the transfer of the final flan or tart a much simpler process.

Roll the pastry out on a lightly floured surface ensuring that it is a few inches larger than the flan case. Wrap the

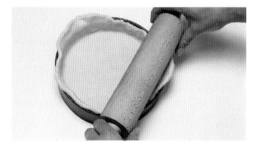

pastry around the rolling pin, lift and place in the tin. Carefully ease the pastry into the base and sides of the tin. Allow to rest for a few minutes then trim the edge with a sharp knife or by rolling a rolling pin across the top of the tin.

Baking Blind

The term baking blind means that the pastry case needs to be cooked without the filling, resulting in a crisp pastry shell that is either partially or fully cooked depending on whether the filling needs any cooking. Pastry shells can be prepared ahead of time, as they last for several days if stored correctly in an airtight container or longer if frozen.

To bake blind, line the tin or dish with the prepared pastry and allow to rest in the refrigerator for 30 minutes. This will help to minimise shrinkage while it is being cooked. Then, lightly prick the base all over with a fork (do not do this if the filling is runny). Brush with a little beaten egg if desired or simply line the case with a large square of greaseproof paper, big enough to cover both the base and sides. Fill with either ceramic baking beans or dried beans. Place on a baking sheet and bake in a preheated oven, generally at 200°C/400°F/Gas Mark 6, remembering that ovens can take at least 15 minutes to reach this heat. Cook for 10–12 minutes, then remove from the oven and discard the paper and beans. Return to the oven and continue to cook for a further 5–10 minutes depending on whether the filling needs cooking.

Covering a Pie Dish

To cover a pie, roll out the pastry until it is about two inches larger than the circumference of the dish. Cut a 2.5 cm/1 inch strip from around the outside of the pastry and then moisten the edge of the pie dish you are using. Place the strip on the edge of the dish and brush with water or beaten egg. Generously fill the pie dish until the surface is slightly rounded. Using the rolling pin, lift the remaining pastry and cover the pie dish. Press together to seal. Using a sharp knife, trim off any excess pastry from around the edges. Try to avoid brushing the edges of the pastry, especially puff pastry as this prevents the pastry rising evenly. Make a small hole in the centre of the pie to allow the steam to escape.

The edges of the pie can be forked by pressing the back of a fork around the edge of the pie, or instead crimp by pinching the edge crust with thumb and index finger. Further decorate by putting leaves and berries made out of leftover pastry on top of the pie, then brush the top with beaten egg.

Lining Cake Tins

If a recipe states that the tin needs lining, do not be tempted to ignore this. Rich fruit cakes and other cakes that take a long time to cook benefit from the tin being lined so that the edges and base do not burn or dry out. Greaseproof or baking parchment paper is ideal for this. It is a good idea to have the paper at least double thickness, or preferably 3–4 thicknesses. Sponge cakes and other cakes that are cooked in 30 minutes or less are also better if the bases are lined as it is far easier to remove them from the tin.

The best way to line a round or square tin is to lightly draw around the base and then cut just inside the markings so it sits easily inside the tin. Next, lightly oil the paper so it easily peels away from the cake. If the sides of the tin also need to be lined, then cut a strip of paper long enough for the tin. This can be measured by wrapping a piece of string around the rim of the tin. Once again, lightly oil the paper, push

against the tin and oil once more as this will hold the paper to the sides of the tin. Steamed puddings usually need only a disc of greaseproof paper at the bottom of the dish.

Hints for Successful Baking

Ensure that the ingredients are accurately measured. A cake that has too much flour or insufficient egg will be dry and crumbly. Too much raising agent will mean that the cake will rise too quickly and then sink. Insufficient raising agent means the cake will not rise in the first place.

Ensure that the oven is preheated to the correct temperature – it can take 10 minutes to reach 180°C/350°F/ Gas Mark 4. You may find that an oven thermometer is a good investment. Cakes are best if cooked in the centre of the oven. Do try to avoid the temptation to open the oven door at the beginning as a draft can make the cake sink. If using a fan oven, refer to the manufacturer's instructions, as they normally cook 10-20° hotter than conventional ovens.

Check that the cake is thoroughly cooked by removing from the oven and inserting a clean skewer. Leave for 30 seconds and remove. If the skewer is completely clean then the cake is cooked; if there is a little mixture left on the skewer then return to the oven for a few minutes.

Other problems that you may encounter are insufficient creaming of the fat and sugar or a curdled creamed mixture (which will result in a densely textured and often fairly solid cake). Flour that has not been folded in carefully enough or has not been mixed with enough raising agent may also result in a fairly heavy consistency. Another tip to be aware of (especially when cooking with fruit) is that if the consistency is too soft, the cake will not be able to support the fruit and it will sink to the bottom.

Finally, when you take your cake out of the oven, unless the recipe states that it should be left in the tin until cold, leave for a few minutes and then loosen the edges and turn out on to a wire rack to cool. Cakes that are left in the tin for too long tend to sink or slightly overcook. When storing, make sure the cake is completely cold before placing it into an airtight tin or plastic container.

Pies, Savoury Flans & Pizzas

You may not have remembered the savoury side of things when you thought of 'baking' but there is a world of delicious pies, quiches and tarts that can be created, using all kinds of fillings such as meat, fish, egg, cheese and vegetables and various types of pastry. Why not practise your baking skills with a Stilton, Tomato & Courgette Quiche or a rich Beef & Red Wine Pie?

Smoked Haddock Tart

1 Preheat the oven to 190°C/375°F/Gas Mark 5. Sift the flour and salt into a large bowl. Add the fats and mix lightly. Using the fingertips rub into the flour until the mixture resembles breadcrumbs.

2 Sprinkle 1 tablespoon of cold water into the mixture and, with a knife, start bringing the dough together. It may be necessary to use your hands for the final stage. If the dough does not form a ball instantly, add a little more water. Put the pastry in a polythene bag and chill for at least 30 minutes.

3 On a lightly floured surface, roll out the pastry and use to line an 18 cm/7 inch lightly oiled quiche or flan tin. Prick the base all over with a fork and bake blind in the preheated oven for 15 minutes.

4 Carefully remove the pastry from the oven and brush with a little of the beaten egg. Return to the oven for a further 5 minutes, then place the fish in the pastry case.

5 For the filling, beat together the eggs and cream. Add the mustard, black pepper and cheese and pour over the fish.

6 Sprinkle with the chives and bake for 35–40 minutes or until the filling is golden brown and set in the centre. Serve hot or cold with the lemon and tomato wedges and salad leaves.

Ingredients　　　　SERVES 4

Shortcrust pastry:

150 g/5 oz plain flour
pinch of salt
25 g/1 oz lard or white vegetable fat, cut into small cubes
40 g/1½ oz butter or hard margarine, cut into small cubes

For the filling:

225 g/8 oz smoked haddock, skinned and cubed
2 large eggs, beaten
300 ml/½ pint double cream
1 tsp Dijon mustard
freshly ground black pepper
125 g/4 oz Gruyère cheese, grated
1 tbsp freshly snipped chives

To serve:

lemon wedges
tomato wedges
fresh green salad leaves

2

4

5

Stilton, Tomato & Courgette Quiche

1 Preheat the oven to 190°C/375°F/Gas Mark 5. On a lightly floured surface, roll out the pastry and use to line an 18 cm/7 inch lightly oiled quiche or flan tin, trimming any excess pastry with a knife.

2 Prick the base all over with a fork and bake blind in the preheated oven for 15 minutes. Remove the pastry from the oven and brush with a little of the beaten egg. Return to the oven for a further 5 minutes.

3 Heat the butter in a frying pan and gently fry the onion and courgette for about 4 minutes until soft and starting to brown. Transfer into the pastry case.

4 Sprinkle the Stilton over evenly and top with the halved cherry tomatoes. Beat together the eggs and crème fraîche and season to taste with salt and pepper.

5 Pour the filling into the pastry case and bake in the oven for 35–40 minutes, or until the filling is golden brown and set in the centre. Serve the quiche hot or cold.

Ingredients   SERVES 4

1 quantity shortcrust pastry
  (see page 12)
25 g/1 oz butter
1 onion, peeled and finely chopped
1 courgette, trimmed and sliced
125 g/4 oz Stilton cheese, crumbled
6 cherry tomatoes, halved
2 large eggs, beaten
200 ml tub crème fraîche
salt and freshly ground black pepper

Food fact

Stilton is a very traditional British cheese which often makes an appearance on the cheese board or served with a ploughman's lunch. It gets much of its full, pungent flavour from its veins (created from the steel wires which are inserted into the cheese during the maturing process). It is worth looking for a piece of Stilton with lots of veins that has been matured for longer.

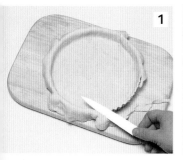

French Onion Tart

1   Preheat the oven to 200°C/400°F/Gas Mark 6. Place the butter in the freezer for 30 minutes. Sift the flour and salt into a large bowl. Remove the butter from the freezer and grate using the coarse side of a grater, dipping the butter in the flour every now and again, which will make it easier to grate. Mix the butter into the flour, using a knife, making sure all the butter is coated thoroughly with flour. Add 2 tablespoons of cold water and continue to mix. Use your hands to complete the mixing. Add a little more water if needed to leave a clean bowl. Place the pastry in a polythene bag and chill in the refrigerator for 30 minutes.

2   Heat the oil in a large frying pan, then fry the onions for 10 minutes, stirring occasionally until softened. Stir in the white wine vinegar and sugar. Increase the heat and stir frequently for another 4–5 minutes until the onions turn a deep caramel colour. Cook for another 5 minutes, then reserve to cool.

3   On a lightly floured surface, roll out the pastry to a 35.5 cm/ 14 inch circle. Wrap over a rolling pin and move the circle on to a baking sheet. Sprinkle half the cheese over the pastry, leaving a 5 cm/2 inch border around the edge, then spoon the caramelised onions over the cheese. Fold the uncovered pastry over the edge of the filling to form a rim and brush it with beaten egg or milk. Season to taste with salt and pepper. Sprinkle over the remaining Cheddar and bake for 20–25 minutes. Transfer to a large plate and serve immediately.

Ingredients   SERVES 4

Quick flaky pastry:
125 g/4 oz butter
175 g/6 oz plain flour
pinch of salt

For the filling:

2 tbsp olive oil
4 large onions, peeled and
    thinly sliced
3 tbsp white wine vinegar
2 tbsp muscovado sugar
a little beaten egg or milk
175 g/6 oz Cheddar cheese, grated
salt and freshly ground black pepper

Tasty tip

For a milder, nutty taste, substitute the Cheddar cheese for Gruyère and grate a little nutmeg over the layer of cheese.

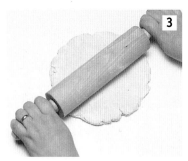

Parsnip Tatin

1 Preheat the oven to 200°C/400°F/Gas Mark 6. Heat the butter in a 20.5 cm/8 inch frying pan.

2 Add the parsnips, arranging the cut side down with the narrow ends towards the centre.

3 Sprinkle the parsnips with sugar and cook for 15 minutes, turning halfway through, until golden.

4 Add the apple juice and bring to the boil. Remove the pan from the heat.

5 On a lightly floured surface, roll the pastry out to a size slightly larger than the frying pan.

6 Position the pastry over the parsnips and press down slightly to enclose the parsnips.

7 Bake in the preheated oven for 20–25 minutes until the parsnips and pastry are golden.

8 Invert a warm serving plate over the pan and carefully turn the pan over to flip the tart on to the plate. Serve immediately.

Ingredients   SERVES 4

1 quantity shortcrust pastry
  (see page 12)

For the filling:
50 g/2 oz butter
8 small parsnips, peeled and halved
1 tbsp brown sugar
75 ml/3 fl oz apple juice

Food fact

In many parts of Europe parsnips are unpopular. Indeed, in Italy they feed them to the pigs. However, parsnips are great winter warmers especially when mashed with potatoes.

Tasty tip

This dish is delicious served warm with a Greek salad. Feta cheese is one of the main ingredients in Greek salad and, because of its salty taste, it tastes particularly good with the creamy flavour of parsnips in this recipe.

3

6

8

Garlic Wild Mushroom Galettes

1 Preheat the oven to 220°C/425°F/Gas Mark 7. On a lightly floured surface roll out the chilled pastry very thinly. Cut out six 15 cm/6 inch circles and place on a lightly oiled baking sheet.

2 Thinly slice the onion, then divide into rings and reserve.

3 Thinly slice the chilli and slice the garlic into wafer-thin slivers. Add to the onions and reserve.

4 Wipe or lightly rinse the mushrooms. Halve or quarter any large mushrooms and keep the small ones whole.

5 Heat the butter in a frying pan and sauté the onion, chilli and garlic gently for about 3 minutes. Add the mushrooms and cook for about 5 minutes, or until beginning to soften.

6 Stir the parsley into the mushroom mixture and drain off any excess liquid.

7 Pile the mushroom mixture on to the pastry circles within 5 mm/¼ inch of the edge. Arrange the sliced mozzarella cheese on top.

8 Bake in the preheated oven for 12–15 minutes, or until golden brown and serve with the tomatoes and salad.

Ingredients   SERVES 6

quantity quick flaky pastry
(see page 16), chilled
1 onion, peeled
1 red chilli, deseeded
2 garlic cloves, peeled
275 g/10 oz mixed mushrooms e.g.
    oyster, chestnuts, morels, ceps
    and chanterelles
25 g/1 oz butter
2 tbsp freshly chopped parsley
125 g/4 oz mozzarella cheese, sliced

To serve:
cherry tomatoes
mixed green salad leaves

Helpful hint
Many supermarkets now stock a variety of wild mushrooms, all of which can be used in this recipe. It is important to maintain as much of the flavour of the mushrooms as possible, so do not peel mushrooms unless they appear old or tough. Either rinse lightly if covered with small pieces of soil or wipe well, trim the stalks and use.

Beef & Red Wine Pie

1 Preheat the oven to 200°C/400°F/Gas Mark 6. Toss the beef cubes in the seasoned flour.

2 Heat the oil in a large heavy-based frying pan. Fry the beef in batches for about 5 minutes until golden brown. Return all of the beef to the pan and add the onions, garlic and thyme. Fry for about 10 minutes, stirring occasionally. If the beef begins to stick, add a little water.

3 Add the red wine and stock and bring to the boil. Stir in the Worcestershire sauce, tomato ketchup and bay leaves. Cover and simmer on a very low heat for about 1 hour or until the beef is tender.

4 Heat the butter and gently sauté the mushrooms until golden brown. Add to the stew. Simmer uncovered for a further 15 minutes. Remove the bay leaves. Spoon the beef into a 1.1 litre/2 pint pie dish and reserve.

5 Roll out the pastry on a lightly floured surface. Cut out the lid to 5 mm/¼ inch wider than the dish. Brush the rim with the beaten egg and lay the pastry lid on top. Press to seal, then knock the edges with the back of the knife to seal further. Cut a slit in the lid and brush with the beaten egg or milk to glaze. Bake in the preheated oven for 30 minutes, or until golden brown. Garnish with the sprig of parsley and serve immediately.

Ingredients   SERVES 4

1 quantity quick flaky pastry (see page 16), chilled
700 g/1½ lb stewing beef, cubed
4 tbsp seasoned plain flour
2 tbsp sunflower oil
2 onions, peeled and chopped
2 garlic cloves, peeled and crushed
1 tbsp freshly chopped thyme
300 ml/½ pint red wine
150 ml/¼ pint beef stock
1–2 tsp Worcestershire sauce
2 tbsp tomato ketchup
2 bay leaves
a knob of butter
225 g/8 oz button mushrooms
beaten egg or milk, to glaze
sprig of parsley, to garnish

Helpful hint

Shortcrust or puff pastry could also be used to top the pie in this recipe. It is important though, whichever pastry is used, to brush the pie with beaten egg or milk before baking, as this will result in an appetising golden crust.

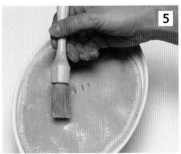

Moroccan Lamb with Apricots

1 Preheat the oven to 190°C/375°F/Gas Mark 5. Pound the ginger, garlic, cardamom and cumin to a paste with a pestle and mortar. Heat 1 tablespoon of the oil in a large frying pan and fry the spice paste for 3 minutes. Remove and reserve.

2 Add the remaining oil and fry the lamb in batches for about 5 minutes, until golden brown. Return all the lamb to the pan and add the onions and spice paste. Fry for 10 minutes, stirring occasionally. Add the chopped tomatoes, cover and simmer for 15 minutes. Add the apricots and chickpeas and simmer for a further 15 minutes.

3 Lightly oil a round 18 cm/7 inch spring form cake tin. Lay one sheet of filo pastry in the base of the tin, allowing the excess to fall over the sides. Brush with melted butter, then layer five more sheets in the tin and brush each one with butter. Spoon in the filling and level the surface. Layer half the remaining filo sheets on top, again brushing each with butter. Fold the overhanging pastry over the top of the filling. Brush the remaining sheet with butter and scrunch up and place on top of the pie so that the whole pie is completely covered. Brush with melted butter once more.

4 Bake in the preheated oven for 45 minutes, then reserve for 10 minutes. Unclip the tin and remove the pie. Sprinkle with the nutmeg, garnish with the dill sprigs and serve.

Ingredients   SERVES 6

5 cm/2 inch piece root ginger,
   peeled and grated
3 garlic cloves, peeled and crushed
1 tsp ground cardamom
1 tsp ground cumin
2 tbsp olive oil
450 g/1 lb lamb neck fillet, cubed
1 large red onion, peeled
   and chopped
400 g can chopped tomatoes
125 g/4 oz ready-to-eat
   dried apricots
400 g can chickpeas, drained
7 large sheets filo pastry
50 g/2 oz butter, melted
pinch of nutmeg
dill sprigs, to garnish

Food fact

Ready-prepared filo pastry is sold rolled in wafer-thin sheets and is available from most supermarkets and good grocers.

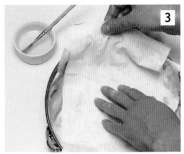

Bacon, Mushroom & Cheese Puffs

1   Preheat the oven to 200 C/400 F/Gas Mark 6. Heat the olive oil in a large frying pan. Add the mushrooms and bacon and fry for 6–8 minutes until golden in colour. Stir in the parsley, season to taste with salt and pepper and allow to cool.

2   Roll the sheet of pastry a little thinner on a lightly floured surface to a 30.5 cm/12 inch square. Cut the pastry into four equal squares.

3   Stir the grated Emmenthal cheese into the mushroom mixture. Spoon a quarter of the mixture on to one half of each square.

4   Brush the edges of the square with a little of the beaten egg. Fold over the pastry to form a triangular parcel. Seal the edges well and place on a lightly oiled baking sheet. Repeat until the squares are done.

5   Make shallow slashes in the top of the pastry with a knife. Brush the parcels with the remaining beaten egg and cook in the preheated oven for 20 minutes, or until puffy and golden brown.

6   Serve warm or cold, garnished with the salad leaves and served with tomatoes

Ingredients   SERVES 4

1 tbsp olive oil
225 g/8 oz field mushrooms, wiped
    and roughly chopped
225 g/8 oz rindless streaky bacon,
    roughly chopped
2 tbsp freshly chopped parsley
salt and freshly ground black pepper
350 g/12 oz ready-rolled puff pastry
    sheets, thawed if frozen
25 g/1 oz Emmenthal cheese, grated
1 medium egg, beaten
salad leaves such as rocket or
    watercress, to garnish
tomatoes, to serve

Tasty tip

The Emmenthal cheese in this recipe can be substituted for any other cheese, but for best results use a cheese such as Cheddar which, like Emmenthal, melts easily. The bacon can also be substituted for slices of sweeter cured hams such as pancetta, speck, Parma or prosciutto.

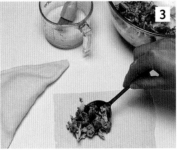

Fennel & Caramelised Shallot Tartlets

1   Preheat the oven to 200°C/400°F/Gas Mark 6. Sift the flour into a bowl, then rub in the butter, using the fingertips. Stir in the cheese, then add the egg yolk with about 2 tablespoons of cold water. Mix to a firm dough, then knead lightly. Wrap in clingfilm and chill in the refrigerator for 30 minutes.

2   Roll out the pastry on a lightly floured surface and use to line six 10 cm/4 inch individual flan tins or patty tins that are about 2 cm/$^3/_4$ inch deep.

3   Line the pastry cases with greaseproof paper and fill with baking beans or rice. Bake blind in the preheated oven for about 10 minutes, then remove the paper and beans.

4   Heat the oil in a frying pan, add the shallots and fennel and fry gently for 5 minutes. Sprinkle with the sugar and cook for a further 10 minutes, stirring occasionally until lightly caramelised. Reserve until cooled.

5   Beat together the egg and cream and season to taste with salt and pepper. Divide the shallot mixture between the pastry cases. Pour over the egg mixture and sprinkle with the cheese and cinnamon. Bake for 20 minutes, until golden and set. Serve with the salad leaves.

Ingredients   SERVES 6
Cheese pastry:
175 g/6 oz plain white flour
75 g/3 oz slightly salted butter
50 g/2 oz Gruyère cheese, grated
1 small egg yolk

For the filling:
2 tbsp olive oil
225 g/8 oz shallots,
    peeled and halved
1 fennel bulb, trimmed and sliced
1 tsp soft brown sugar
1 medium egg
150 ml/$^1/_4$ pint double cream
salt and freshly ground black pepper
25 g/1 oz Gruyère cheese, grated
$^1/_2$ tsp ground cinnamon
mixed salad leaves, to serve

Tasty tip
If wanted, you could add a generous grating of nutmeg to the pie filling in step 5 as this complements the creamy cheese filling.

Roasted Vegetable Pie

1 Preheat the oven to 220°C/425°F/Gas Mark 7. Sift the flour and salt into a bowl, add the fats and mix lightly. Use the fingertips to rub until the mixture resembles breadcrumbs. Stir in the herbes de Provence. Sprinkle over a tablespoon of cold water and, with a knife, start bringing the dough together. If necessary use your hands for the final stage. If the dough does not form a ball instantly, add a little more water. Place in a polythene bag and chill for 30 minutes. Place the peppers on a baking tray and sprinkle with 1 tablespoon of oil. Roast for 20 minutes or until the skins start to blacken. Brush the other vegetables with oil and place on a baking tray. Roast with the peppers for 20 minutes. Place the peppers in a polythene bag and leave the skin to loosen for 5 minutes. When cool enough, peel off the skins.

2 Roll out half the pastry on a lightly floured surface and use to line a 20.5 cm/8 inch round pie dish. Line with greaseproof paper and fill with baking beans or rice and bake blind for 10 minutes. Remove the beans and paper, then brush the base with a little of the beaten egg. Return to the oven for 5 minutes, then layer the cooked vegetables and the cheese in the case, seasoning each layer. Roll out the remaining pastry and cut out the lid 5 mm/$^1/_4$ inch wider than the dish. Brush the rim with the egg and lay the pastry lid on top, pressing to seal. Knock the edges with the back of a knife. Cut a slit in the lid and brush with the egg. Bake for 30 minutes. Transfer to a large serving dish, garnish with sprigs of herbs and serve immediately.

Ingredients   SERVES 4

225 g/8 oz plain flour
pinch of salt
50 g/2 oz white vegetable fat or lard,
    cut into squares
50 g/2 oz butter, cut into squares
2 tsp herbes de Provence
1 red pepper, deseeded and halved
1 green pepper, deseeded
    and halved
1 yellow pepper, deseeded
    and halved
3 tbsp extra virgin olive oil
1 aubergine, trimmed and sliced
1 courgette, trimmed and halved
    lengthways
1 leek, trimmed and cut into chunks
1 medium egg, beaten
125 g/4 oz fresh mozzarella
    cheese, sliced
salt and freshly ground black pepper
sprigs of mixed herbs, to garnish

Helpful hint

Look out for buffalo mozzarella because it is the best available.

Chicken & Ham Pie

1 Preheat the oven to 200°C/400°F/Gas Mark 6. Heat the oil in a frying pan and fry the leek and bacon for 4 minutes until soft but not coloured. Transfer to a bowl and reserve.

2 Cut the chicken into bite-sized pieces and add to the leek and bacon. Toss the avocado in the lemon juice, add to the chicken and season to taste with salt and pepper.

3 Roll out half the pastry on a lightly floured surface and use to line an 18 cm/7 inch loose-bottomed deep flan tin. Scoop the chicken mixture into the pastry case.

4 Mix together 1 egg, the yogurt and the chicken stock. Pour the yogurt mixture over the chicken. Roll out the remaining pastry on a lightly floured surface and cut out the lid to 5 mm/¹/₄ inch wider than the dish.

5 Brush the rim with the remaining beaten egg and lay the pastry lid on top, pressing to seal.

6 Knock the edges with the back of a knife to seal further. Cut a slit in the lid and brush with the egg.

7 Sprinkle with the poppy seeds and bake in the preheated oven for about 30 minutes, or until the pastry is golden brown. Serve with the onion and mixed salad leaves.

Ingredients   SERVES 6

2 quantities shortcrust pastry,
  (see page 12)
1 tbsp olive oil
1 leek, trimmed and sliced
175 g/6 oz piece of bacon, cut into
  small dice
225 g/8 oz cooked boneless
  chicken meat
2 avocados, peeled, pitted and chopped
1 tbsp lemon juice
salt and freshly ground black pepper
2 large eggs, beaten
150 ml/¹/₄ pint natural yogurt
4 tbsp chicken stock
1 tbsp poppy seeds

To serve:

sliced red onion
mixed salad leaves

Helpful hint

Corn-fed or free-range chickens are more flavoursome and tender than standard supermarket birds and they are worth the extra money.

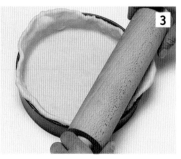

Fish Puff Tart

1 Preheat the oven to 220°C/425°F/Gas Mark 7. On a lightly floured surface roll out the pastry into a 20.5 x 25.5 cm/8 x 10 inch rectangle.

2 Draw an 18 x 23 cm/7 x 9 inch rectangle in the centre of the pastry, to form a 2.5 cm/1 inch border. Be careful not to cut through the pastry.

3 Lightly cut criss-cross patterns in the border of the pastry with a knife.

4 Place the fish on a chopping board and, with a sharp knife, skin the cod and smoked haddock. Cut into thin slices.

5 Spread the pesto evenly over the bottom of the pastry case with the back of a spoon.

6 Arrange the fish, tomatoes and cheese in the pastry case and brush the pastry with the beaten egg.

7 Bake the tart in the preheated oven for 20–25 minutes, until the pastry is well risen, puffed and golden brown. Garnish with the chopped parsley and serve immediately.

Ingredients
SERVES 4

350 g/12 oz prepared puff pastry,
  thawed if frozen
150 g/5 oz smoked haddock
150 g/5 oz cod
1 tbsp pesto sauce
2 tomatoes, sliced
125 g/4 oz goat's cheese, sliced
1 medium egg, beaten
freshly chopped parsley, to garnish

Food fact

The Scottish name for smoked haddock is finnan haddie, named after the Scottish fishing village of Findon near Aberdeen. Smoked haddock has been a favourite breakfast dish in Findon and the rest of Scotland for many years. Although this type of fish was traditionally caught and smoked (sometimes over peat fires) in Scotland, nowadays the fish is produced in New England and other eastern coastal states of the United States.

Spinach, Pine Nut & Mascarpone Pizza

1   Preheat the oven to 220°C/425°F/ Gas Mark 7. Sift the flour
    and salt into a bowl and stir in the yeast. Make a well in the
    centre and gradually add the water and oil to form a soft dough.

2   Knead the dough on a floured surface for about 5 minutes until
    smooth and elastic. Place in a lightly oiled bowl and cover with
    clingfilm. Leave to rise in a warm place for 1 hour.

3   Knock the pizza dough with your fist a few times, shape and
    roll out thinly on a lightly floured board. Place on a lightly
    floured baking sheet and lift the edge to make a little rim. Place
    another baking sheet into the preheated oven to heat up.

4   Heat half the oil in a frying pan and gently fry the onion and
    garlic until soft and starting to change colour.

5   Squeeze out any excess water from the spinach and finely
    chop. Add to the onion and garlic with the remaining olive oil.
    Season to taste with salt and pepper.

6   Spread the passata on the pizza dough and top with the
    spinach mixture. Mix the mascarpone with the pine nuts and
    dot over the pizza.

7   Slide the pizza on to the hot baking sheet and bake for 15–20
    minutes. Transfer to a large plate and serve immediately.

Ingredients   SERVES 2–4

Basic pizza dough:
225 g/8 oz strong plain flour
$^1/_2$ tsp salt
$^1/_4$ tsp quick-acting dried yeast
150 ml/$^1/_4$ pint warm water
1 tbsp extra virgin olive oil

For the topping:
3 tbsp olive oil
1 large red onion, peeled
   and chopped
2 garlic cloves, peeled and
   finely sliced
450 g/1 lb frozen spinach leaves,
   thawed and drained
salt and freshly ground black pepper
3 tbsp passata
125 g/4 oz mascarpone cheese
1 tbsp toasted pine nuts

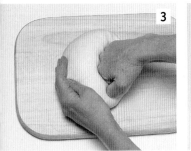

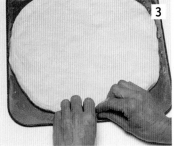

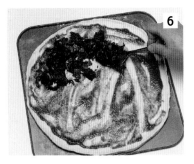

Roquefort, Parma & Rocket Pizza

1   Preheat the oven to 220°C/425°F/Gas Mark 7. Roll the pizza dough out on a lightly floured board to form a 25.5 cm/10 inch round.

2   Lightly cover the dough and reserve while making the sauce. Place a baking sheet in the preheated oven to heat up.

3   Place all of the tomato sauce ingredients in a large heavy-based saucepan and slowly bring to the boil.

4   Cover and simmer for 15 minutes, uncover and cook for a further 10 minutes until the sauce has thickened and reduced by half.

5   Spoon the tomato sauce over the shaped pizza dough. Place on the hot baking sheet and bake for 10 minutes.

6   Remove the pizza from the oven and top with the Roquefort and Parma ham, then bake for a further 10 minutes.

7   Toss the rocket in the olive oil and pile on to the pizza. Sprinkle with the Parmesan cheese and serve immediately.

Ingredients   SERVES 2–4

1 quantity pizza dough (see page 36)

Basic tomato sauce:
400 g can chopped tomatoes
2 garlic cloves, peeled and crushed
grated rind of $^1/_2$ lime
2 tbsp extra virgin olive oil
2 tbsp freshly chopped basil
$^1/_2$ tsp sugar
salt and freshly ground black pepper

For the topping
125 g/4 oz Roquefort cheese,
    cut into chunks
6 slices Parma ham
50 g/2 oz rocket leaves, rinsed
1 tbsp extra virgin olive oil
50 g/2 oz Parmesan cheese,
    freshly shaved

Food fact

To make a thin and crispy-based pizza, roll the dough out to a 12-inch round in step 1, then continue as demonstrated.

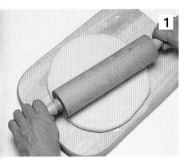

Breads, Scones & Teabreads

There is nothing much better than the smell of fresh bread wafting through the house. Follow easy step-by-step instructions to make basics such as the Classic White Loaf or delicious flavoured breads including Rosemary & Olive Focaccia and Spicy Filled Naan Bread. Or spoil yourself with something sweet like the tasty Fruity Apple Tea Bread.

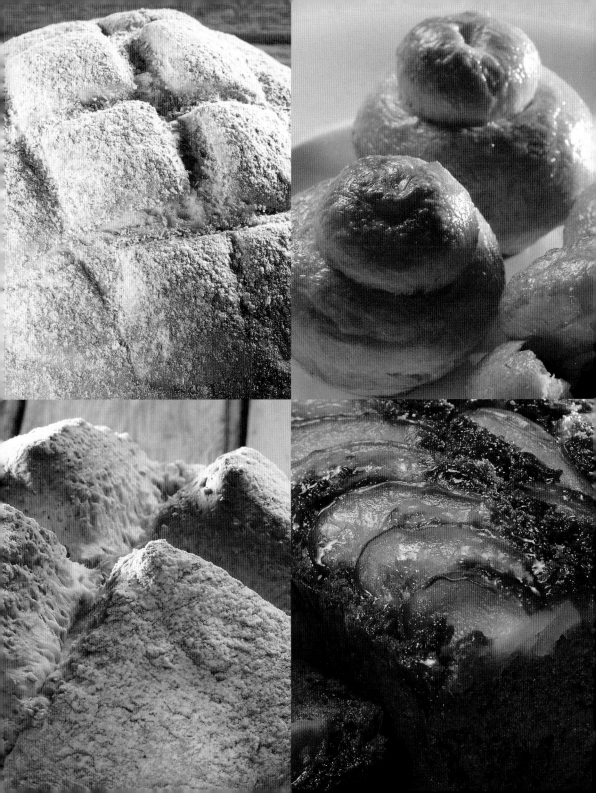

Classic White Loaf

1 Preheat the oven to 220°C/425°F/Gas Mark 7, 15 minutes before baking. Oil and line the base of a 900 g/2 lb loaf tin with greaseproof paper. Sift the flour and salt into a large bowl. Rub in the butter, then stir in the sugar and yeast. Make a well in the centre.

2 Add the milk and the warm water to the dry ingredients. Mix to a soft dough, adding a little more water if needed. Turn out the dough and knead on a lightly floured surface for 10 minutes, or until smooth and elastic.

3 Place the dough in an oiled bowl, cover with clingfilm or a clean tea towel and leave in a warm place to rise for 1 hour, or until doubled in size. Knead again for a minute or two to knock out the air.

4 Shape the dough into an oblong and place in the prepared tin. Cover with oiled clingfilm and leave to rise for a further 30 minutes or until the dough reaches the top of the tin. Dredge the top of the loaf with flour or brush with the egg glaze and scatter with kibbled wheat if making the wholemeal version. Bake the loaf on the middle shelf of the preheated oven for 15 minutes.

5 Turn down the oven to 200°C/400°F/Gas Mark 6. Bake the loaf for a further 20–25 minutes, or until well risen and hollow sounding when tapped underneath. Turn out, cool on a wire rack and serve.

Ingredients

MAKES 1 x 900 G LOAF

700 g/1¹/₂ lb strong white flour
1 tbsp salt
25 g/1 oz butter, cubed
1 tsp caster sugar
2 tsp easy-blend dried yeast
150 ml/¹/₄ pint milk
300 ml/¹/₂ pint warm water
1 tbsp plain flour, to dredge

Light wholemeal variation:

450 g/1 lb strong wholemeal flour
225 g/8 oz strong white flour
beaten egg, to glaze
1 tbsp kibbled wheat, to finish

Tasty tip

Nothing beats a freshly-cooked loaf of white bread. While the bread is still warm, spread generously with fresh butter and eat.

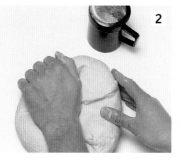

Mixed Grain Bread

1 Preheat the oven to 220°C/425°F/Gas Mark 7, 15 minutes before baking. Sift the white flour and salt into a large bowl. Stir in the Granary and rye flours, then rub in the butter until the mixture resembles breadcrumbs. Stir in the yeast, oats and seeds and make a well in the centre.

2 Stir the malt extract into the warm water until dissolved. Add the malt water to the dry ingredients. Mix to a soft dough.

3 Turn the dough out on to a lightly floured surface and knead for 10 minutes, until smooth and elastic.

4 Put in an oiled bowl, cover with clingfilm and leave to rise in a warm place for 1½ hours or until doubled in size.

5 Turn out and knead again for a minute or two to knock out the air.

6 Shape into an oval loaf about 30.5 cm/12 inches long and place on a well-oiled baking sheet. Cover with oiled clingfilm and leave to rise for 40 minutes, or until doubled in size.

7 Brush the loaf with beaten egg and bake in the preheated oven for 35–45 minutes, or until the bread is well risen, browned and sounds hollow when the base is tapped. Leave to cool on a wire rack, then serve.

Ingredients

MAKES 1 LARGE LOAF

350 g/12 oz strong white flour
2 tsp salt
225 g/8 oz strong Granary flour
125 g/4 oz rye flour
25 g/1 oz butter, diced
2 tsp easy-blend dried yeast
25 g/1 oz rolled oats
2 tbsp sunflower seeds
1 tbsp malt extract
450 ml/¾ pint warm water
 (see Helpful hint)
1 medium egg, beaten

Helpful hint

The amount of water you need to add to the dry ingredients in this recipe will depend on the type and brand of flour you use. Add just enough water to make a soft elastic dough.

2

4

7

Quick Brown Bread

1 Preheat the oven to 200°C/400°F/Gas Mark 6, 15 minutes before baking. Oil two 450 g/1 lb loaf tins. Sift the flour, salt and sugar into a large bowl, adding the remaining bran in the sieve. Stir in the yeast, then make a well in the centre. Pour the warm water into the dry ingredients and mix to form a soft dough, adding a little more water if needed. Knead on a lightly floured surface for 10 minutes, until smooth and elastic. Divide in half, shape into two oblongs and place in the tins. Cover with oiled clingfilm and leave in a warm place for 40 minutes, or until risen to the top of the tins.

2 Glaze one loaf with the beaten egg and dust the other loaf generously with the plain flour. Bake the loaves in the preheated oven for 35 minutes or until well risen and lightly browned. Turn out of the tins and return to the oven for 5 minutes to crisp the sides. Cool on a wire rack.

3 For the onion and caraway seed rolls, gently fry the onion in the oil until soft. Reserve until the onions are cool, then stir into the dry ingredients with 1 tablespoon of the caraway seeds. Make the dough as before. Divide the dough into 16 pieces and shape into rolls. Put on two oiled baking trays, cover with oiled clingfilm and prove for 30 minutes.

4 Glaze the rolls with milk and sprinkle with the rest of the seeds. Bake for 25–30 minutes, cool on a wire rack and serve.

Ingredients
MAKES 2 x 1 lb LOAVES

700 g/1$\frac{1}{2}$ lb strong wholemeal flour
2 tsp salt
$\frac{1}{2}$ tsp caster sugar
7 g/$\frac{1}{4}$ oz sachet easy-blend
    dried yeast
450 ml/$\frac{3}{4}$ pint warm water

To finish:
beaten egg, to glaze
1 tbsp plain white flour, to dust

Onion & caraway seed rolls:
1 small onion, peeled and finely
    chopped
1 tbsp olive oil
2 tbsp caraway seeds
milk, to glaze

Rustic Country Bread

1 For the starter, sift the flour into a bowl. Stir in the yeast and make a well in the centre. Pour in the warm water and mix with a fork. Transfer to a saucepan, cover with a clean tea towel and leave for 2–3 days at room temperature. Stir the mixture and spray with a little water twice a day.

2 Preheat the oven to 220°C/425°F/Gas Mark 7, 15 minutes before baking. For the dough, mix the flours, salt, sugar and yeast in a bowl. Add 225 ml/8 fl oz of the starter, the oil and the warm water. Mix to a soft dough.

3 Knead on a lightly floured surface for 10 minutes until smooth and elastic. Put in an oiled bowl, cover and leave to rise in a warm place for about 1½ hours, or until doubled in size.

4 Turn the dough out and knead for a minute or two. Shape into a round loaf and place on an oiled baking sheet. Cover with oiled clingfilm and leave to rise for 1 hour, or until doubled in size.

5 Dust the loaf with flour, then using a sharp knife make several slashes across the top of the loaf. Slash across the loaf in the opposite direction to make a square pattern.

6 Bake in the preheated oven for 40–45 minutes, or until golden brown and hollow-sounding when tapped underneath. Cool on a wire rack and serve.

Ingredients
MAKES 1 LARGE LOAF

Sourdough starter:
225 g/8 oz strong white flour
2 tsp easy-blend dried yeast
300 ml/½ pint warm water

Bread dough:
350 g/12 oz strong white flour
25 g/1 oz rye flour
1½ tsp salt
½ tsp caster sugar
1 tsp dried yeast
1 tsp sunflower oil
175 ml/6 fl oz warm water

To finish:
2 tsp plain flour
2 tsp rye flour

Helpful hint
Put the remaining starter in a pan, stir in 125 ml/4 fl oz of warm water and 125 g/4 oz strong white flour. Stir twice a day for 2–3 days and use as a starter for another loaf.

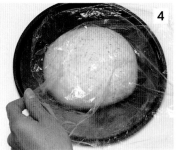

Soft Dinner Rolls

1 Preheat the oven to 220°C/425°F/Gas Mark 7, 15 minutes before baking. Gently heat the butter, sugar and milk in a saucepan until the butter has melted and the sugar has dissolved. Cool until tepid. Sift the flour and salt into a bowl, stir in the yeast and make a well in the centre. Reserve 1 tablespoon of the beaten eggs. Add the rest to the dry ingredients with the milk mixture. Mix to form a soft dough.

2 Knead the dough on a lightly floured surface for 10 minutes until smooth and elastic. Put in an oiled bowl, cover with clingfilm and leave in a warm place to rise for 1 hour, or until doubled in size. Knead again for a minute or two, then divide into 16 pieces. Shape into plaits, snails, clover leaves and cottage buns (see Helpful Hints). Place on two oiled baking sheets, cover with oiled clingfilm and leave to rise for 30 minutes, until doubled in size.

3 Mix the reserved beaten egg with the milk and brush over the rolls. Sprinkle some with sea salt, others with poppy seeds and leave some plain. Bake in the preheated oven for about 20 minutes, or until golden and hollow sounding when tapped underneath. Transfer to a wire rack. Cover with a clean tea towel while cooling to keep the rolls soft, then serve.

Ingredients MAKES 16

50 g/2 oz butter
1 tbsp caster sugar
225 ml/8 fl oz milk
550 g/1¼ lbs strong white flour
1½ tsp salt
2 tsp easy-blend dried yeast
2 medium eggs, beaten

To glaze & finish:

2 tbsp milk
1 tsp sea salt
2 tsp poppy seeds

Helpful hint

For clover leaf rolls, divide into three equal pieces and roll each into a ball. Place the balls together in a triangular shape. For cottage buns, divide the dough into two-thirds and one-third pieces. Shape each piece into a round, then put the smaller one on top of the larger one. Push a floured wooden spoon handle or finger through the middle of the top one and into the bottom one to join together.

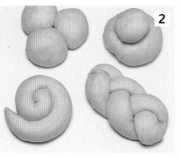

Bagels

1 Preheat the oven to 200°C/400°F/Gas Mark 6, 15 minutes before baking. Sift the flour and salt into a large bowl. Stir in the yeast, then make a well in the centre. Whisk the eggs together with the honey and oil. Add to the dry ingredients with the tepid water and mix to form a soft dough.

2 Knead the dough on a lightly floured surface for 10 minutes until smooth and elastic. Put in a bowl, cover with clingfilm and leave in a warm place to rise for 45 minutes, or until doubled in size.

3 Briefly knead the dough again to knock out the air. Divide into 12 pieces, form each into a 20.5 cm/8 inch roll, curve into a ring and pinch the edges to seal. Put the rings on an oiled baking sheet, cover with oiled clingfilm and leave to rise in a warm place for 20 minutes, or until risen and puffy.

4 Add the caster sugar to a large saucepan of water. Bring to the boil, then drop in the bagels one at a time and poach for 15 seconds. Lift out with a slotted spoon and return to the baking tray.

5 Brush the bagels with beaten egg and sprinkle one third with poppy seeds. Mix together the onion and oil and sprinkle over another third of the bagels. Leave the remaining third plain.

6 Bake in the preheated oven for 12–15 minutes, or until golden brown. Transfer to a wire rack and serve when cool.

Ingredients   SERVES 4

450 g/1 lb strong plain flour
1½ tsp salt
2 tsp easy-blend dried yeast
2 medium eggs
1 tsp clear honey
2 tbsp sunflower oil
250 ml/9 fl oz tepid water

To finish:

1 tbsp caster sugar
beaten egg, to glaze
2 tsp poppy seeds
½ small onion, peeled and
    finely chopped
2 tsp sunflower oil

Tasty tip

Why not try bagels for breakfast? They are delicious filled with cheese and ham or served toasted with scrambled egg. They are also good with smoked salmon and cream cheese.

Sweet Potato Baps

1 Preheat the oven to 200°C/400°F/Gas Mark 6, 15 minutes before baking. Peel the sweet potato and cut into large chunks. Cook in a saucepan of boiling water for 12–15 minutes, or until tender. Drain well and mash with the butter and nutmeg. Stir in the milk, then leave until barely warm.

2 Sift the flour and salt into a large bowl. Stir in the yeast. Make a well in the centre. Add the mashed sweet potato and beaten egg and mix to a soft dough. Add a little more milk if needed, depending on the moisture in the sweet potato.

3 Turn out the dough on to a lightly floured surface and knead for about 10 minutes, or until smooth and elastic. Place in a lightly oiled bowl, cover with clingfilm and leave in a warm place to rise for about 1 hour, or until the dough doubles in size.

4 Turn out the dough and knead for a minute or two until smooth. Divide into 16 pieces, shape into rolls and place on a large oiled baking sheet. Cover with oiled clingfilm and leave to rise for 15 minutes.

5 Brush the rolls with beaten egg, then sprinkle half with rolled oats and leave the rest plain. Bake in the oven for 12–15 minutes, or until the rolls are well risen, lightly browned and sound hollow when the bases are tapped. Transfer to a wire rack and cover with a clean tea towel to keep the crusts soft.

Ingredients MAKES 16

225 g/8 oz sweet potato
15 g/½ oz butter
freshly grated nutmeg
about 200 ml/7 fl oz milk
450 g/1 lb strong white flour
2 tsp salt
7 g/¼ oz sachet easy-blend yeast
1 medium egg, beaten

To finish:

beaten egg, to glaze
1 tbsp rolled oats

Helpful hint

There are many varieties of sweet potato, so be sure to choose the correct potato for this recipe, as their flavours and textures vary. The sweet potato used in this recipe is dark skinned and has a vibrant orange flesh which cooks to a moist texture.

Rosemary & Olive Focaccia

1 Preheat the oven to 200°C/400°F/Gas Mark 6, 15 minutes before baking. Sift the flour, salt and sugar into a large bowl. Stir in the yeast and rosemary. Make a well in the centre.

2 Pour in the warm water and the oil and mix to a soft dough. Turn out on to a lightly floured surface and knead for about 10 minutes, until smooth and elastic.

3 Pat the olives dry on kitchen paper, then gently knead into the dough. Put in an oiled bowl, cover with clingfilm and leave to rise in a warm place for 1$^1/_2$ hours, or until it has doubled in size.

4 Turn out the dough and knead again for a minute or two. Divide in half and roll out each piece to a 25.5 cm/10 inch circle.

5 Transfer to oiled baking sheets, cover with oiled clingfilm and leave to rise for 30 minutes.

6 Using the fingertips, make deep dimples all over the the dough. Drizzle with the oil and sprinkle with sea salt.

7 Bake in the preheated oven for 20–25 minutes, or until risen and golden. Cool on a wire rack and garnish with sprigs of rosemary. Grind over a little black pepper before serving.

Ingredients   MAKES 2 LOAVES

700 g/1$^1/_2$ lb strong white flour
pinch of salt
pinch of caster sugar
7 g/$^1/_4$ oz sachet easy-blend
    dried yeast
2 tsp freshly chopped rosemary
450 ml/$^3/_4$ pint warm water
3 tbsp olive oil
75 g/3 oz pitted black olives,
    roughly chopped
sprigs of rosemary, to garnish

To finish:

3 tbsp olive oil
coarse sea salt
freshly ground black pepper

Tasty tip

You could replace the rosemary with some chopped sun-dried tomatoes. Knead the tomatoes into the dough along with the olives in step 3, then before baking drizzle with the oil and replace the salt with some grated mozzarella cheese.

Spicy Filled Naan Bread

1 Preheat the oven to 220°C/425°F/Gas Mark 7, 15 minutes before baking and place a large baking sheet in it to heat up. Sift the flour and salt into a large bowl. Stir in the yeast and make a well in the centre. Add the ghee or melted butter, honey and the warm water. Mix to a soft dough.

2 Knead the dough on a lightly floured surface, until smooth and elastic. Put in a lightly oiled bowl, cover with clingfilm and leave to rise for 1 hour, or until doubled in size.

3 For the filling, melt the ghee or butter in a frying pan and gently cook the onion for about 5 minutes. Stir in the garlic and spices and season to taste with salt and pepper. Cook for a further 6–7 minutes, until soft. Remove from the heat, stir in 1 tablespoon of water and leave to cool.

4 Briefly knead the dough, then divide into six pieces. Roll out each piece of dough to 12.5 cm/5 inch rounds. Spoon the filling on to one half of each round. Fold over and press the edges together to seal. Re-roll to shape into flat ovals, about 16 cm/6½ inches long. Cover with oiled clingfilm and leave to rise for about 15 minutes.

5 Transfer the breads to the hot baking sheet and cook in the preheated oven for 10–12 minutes, until puffed up and lightly browned. Serve hot.

Ingredients   MAKES 6

400 g/14 oz strong white flour
1 tsp salt
1 tsp easy-blend dried yeast
15 g/½ oz ghee or unsalted butter, melted
1 tsp clear honey
200 ml/7 fl oz warm water

For the filling:

25 g/1 oz ghee or unsalted butter
1 small onion, peeled and finely chopped
1 garlic clove, peeled and crushed
1 tsp ground coriander
1 tsp ground cumin
2 tsp grated fresh root ginger
pinch of chilli powder
pinch of ground cinnamon
salt and freshly ground black pepper

Helpful hint

Ghee is more expensive than other butters but it has a longer life and a much higher smoke point (190°C/375°F). Ghee, therefore, is practical for sautéing and frying.

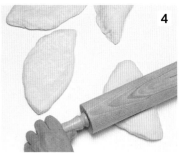

Fruited Brioche Buns

1   Preheat the oven to 220°C/425°F/Gas Mark 7, 15 minutes before baking. Sift the flour and salt into a bowl. Stir in the sugar and yeast. Make a well in the centre. Add the eggs, butter and 2 tablespoons of warm water and mix to a soft dough. Knead the dough on a lightly floured surface for 5 minutes, until smooth and elastic. Put in an oiled bowl, cover with clingfilm and leave to rise in a warm place for 1 hour, or until it has doubled in size. Mix the ingredients for the filling together, cover the bowl and leave to soak while the dough is rising.

2   Re-knead the dough for a minute or two, then divide into 12 pieces. Take 1 piece at a time and flatten three-quarters into a 6.5 cm/2½ inch round. Spoon a little filling in the centre, then pinch the edges together to enclose. Put seam-side down into a well-greased fluted 12-hole bun tin.

3   Shape the smaller piece of dough into a round and place on top of the larger one. Push a finger or floured wooden spoon handle through the middle of the top one and into the bottom one to join them together. Repeat with the remaining balls of dough. Cover the brioche with oiled clingfilm and leave for about 20 minutes, or until well risen.

4   Brush the brioches with beaten egg and bake in the preheated oven for 10–12 minutes, or until golden. Cool on a wire rack and serve.

Ingredients   MAKES 12

225 g/8 oz strong white flour
pinch of salt
1 tbsp caster sugar
7 g/¼ oz sachet easy-blend
   dried yeast
2 large eggs, beaten
50 g/2 oz butter, melted
beaten egg, to glaze

For the filling:

40 g/1½ oz blanched almonds,
   chopped
50 g/2 oz luxury mixed dried fruit
1 tsp light soft brown sugar
2 tsp orange liqueur or brandy

Spiced Apple Doughnuts

1   Sift the flour, salt and 1 teaspoon of the cinnamon into a large bowl. Stir in the yeast and make a well in the centre.

2   Add the milk, butter and egg and mix to a soft dough. Knead on a lightly floured surface for 10 minutes, until smooth and elastic.

3   Divide the dough into eight pieces and shape each into a ball. Put on a floured baking sheet, cover with oiled clingfilm and leave in a warm place for 1 hour, or until doubled in size.

4   To make the filling, put the apples in a saucepan with the sugar, lemon juice and 3 tablespoons of water. Cover and simmer for about 10 minutes, then uncover and cook until fairly dry, stirring occasionally. Mash or blend in a food processor to a purée.

5   Pour enough oil into a deep-fat frying pan to come one third of the way up the pan. Heat the oil to 180°C/350°F, then deep-fry the doughnuts for 1½–2 minutes, until well browned.

6   Drain the doughnuts on kitchen paper, then roll in the caster sugar mixed with the remaining ½ teaspoon of ground cinnamon. Push a thick skewer into the centre to make a hole, then pipe in the apple filling. Serve warm or cold.

Ingredients   MAKES 8

225 g/8 oz strong white flour
½ tsp salt
1½ tsp ground cinnamon
1 tsp easy-blend dried yeast
75 ml/3 fl oz warm milk
25 g/1 oz butter, melted
1 medium egg, beaten
oil, to deep-fry
4 tbsp caster sugar, to coat

For the filling:

2 small eating apples, peeled, cored and chopped
2 tsp soft light brown sugar
2 tsp lemon juice

Tasty tip

These doughnuts are also excellent when filled with pears. Simply replace the 2 apples with 2 pears and continue with the recipe. Look out for Comice pears as they are considered to be amongst the best on the market.

Bacon & Tomato Breakfast Twist

1 Preheat the oven to 200°C/400°F/Gas Mark 6, 15 minutes before baking. Sift the flour and salt into a large bowl. Stir in the yeast and make a well in the centre. Pour in the milk and butter and mix to a soft dough. Knead on a lightly floured surface for 10 minutes, until smooth and elastic. Put in an oiled bowl, cover with clingfilm and leave to rise in a warm place for 1 hour, until doubled in size.

2 Cook the bacon under a hot grill for 5–6 minutes, turning once, until crisp. Leave to cool, then chop roughly .

3 Knead the dough again for a minute or two. Roll it out to a 25.5 x 33 cm/10 x 13 inch rectangle. Cut in half lengthways. Brush lightly with butter, then scatter with the bacon, tomatoes and black pepper, leaving a 1 cm/¹/₂ inch margin around the edges. Brush the edges of the dough with beaten egg, then roll up each rectangle lengthways.

4 Place the two rolls side by side and twist together, pinching the ends to seal. Transfer to an oiled baking sheet and cover loosely with oiled clingfilm. Leave to rise in a warm place for 30 minutes.

5 Brush with the beaten egg and sprinkle with the oatmeal. Bake in the preheated oven for about 30 minutes, or until golden brown and hollow-sounding when tapped on the base. Serve the bread warm in thick slices.

Ingredients   SERVES 8

450 g/1 lb strong plain flour
¹/₂ tsp salt
7 g/¹/₄ oz sachet easy-blend
   dried yeast
300 ml/¹/₂ pint warm milk
15 g/¹/₂ oz butter, melted

For the filling:

225 g/8 oz back bacon, derinded
15 g/¹/₂ oz butter, melted
175 g/6 oz ripe tomatoes, peeled,
   deseeded and chopped
freshly ground black pepper

To finish:

beaten egg, to glaze
2 tsp medium oatmeal

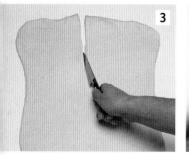

Irish Soda Bread

1   Preheat the oven to 200°C/400°F/Gas Mark 6, 15 minutes before baking. Sift the flour, salt and bicarbonate of soda into a large bowl. Rub in the butter until the mixture resembles fine breadcrumbs. Stir in the oatmeal and make a well in the centre.

2   Mix the honey, buttermilk and milk together and add to the dry ingredients. Mix to a soft dough.

3   Knead the dough on a lightly floured surface for 2–3 minutes, until the dough is smooth. Shape into a 20.5 cm/8 inch round and place on an oiled baking sheet.

4   Thickly dust the top of the bread with flour. Using a sharp knife, cut a deep cross on top, going about halfway through the loaf.

5   Bake in the preheated oven on the middle shelf for 30–35 minutes or until the bread is slightly risen, golden and sounds hollow when tapped underneath. Cool on a wire rack. Eat on the day of making.

6   For a wholemeal soda bread, use all the wholemeal flour instead of the white flour and add an extra tablespoon of milk when mixing together. Dust the top with wholemeal flour and bake.

Ingredients   MAKES 1 LOAF

400 g/14 oz plain white flour,
   plus 1 tbsp for dusting
1 tsp salt
2 tsp bicarbonate of soda
15 g/$^1\!/_2$ oz butter
50 g/2 oz coarse oatmeal
1 tsp clear honey
300 ml/$^1\!/_2$ pint buttermilk
2 tbsp milk

Wholemeal variation:

400 g/14 oz plain wholemeal flour,
   plus 1 tbsp for dusting
1 tbsp milk

Tasty tip

Soda bread relies on the raising agent bicarbonate of soda, which, when combined with the acidic buttermilk, enables the bread to rise. For an unusual Irish soda bread, knead in a handful of currants and 2 tablespoons of caraway seeds in step 3. According to Irish legend, the cross on the top of the bread is intended to scare away the devil.

Traditional Oven Scones

1 Preheat the oven to 220°C/425°F/Gas Mark 7, 15 minutes before baking. Sift the flour, baking powder and salt into a large bowl. Rub in the butter until the mixture resembles fine breadcrumbs. Stir in the sugar and mix in enough milk to give a fairly soft dough.

2 Knead the dough on a lightly floured surface for a few seconds until smooth. Roll out until 2 cm/³/₄ inches thick and stamp out 6.5 cm/2¹/₂ inch rounds with a floured plain cutter.

3 Place on an oiled baking sheet and brush the tops with milk – do not brush it over the sides or the scones will not rise properly. Dust with a little plain flour.

4 Bake in the preheated oven for 12–15 minutes, or until well risen and golden brown. Transfer to a wire rack and serve warm or leave to cool completely. The scones are best eaten on the day of baking but may be kept in an airtight tin for up to 2 days.

5 For lemon and sultana scones, stir in the sultanas and lemon rind with the sugar. Roll out until 2 cm/³/₄ inches thick and cut into eight fingers, 10 x 2.5 cm/4 x 1 inch in size. Bake the scones as before.

Ingredients   MAKES 8

225 g/8 oz self-raising flour
1 tsp baking powder
pinch of salt
40 g/1¹/₂ oz butter, cubed
15 g/¹/₂ oz caster sugar
150 ml/¹/₄ pint milk,
    plus 1 tbsp for brushing
1 tbsp plain flour, to dust

Lemon & sultana scone variation:

50 g/2 oz sultanas
finely grated rind of ¹/₂ lemon
beaten egg, to glaze

Cheese-crusted Potato Scones

1. Preheat the oven to 220°C/425°F/Gas Mark 7, 15 minutes before baking. Sift the flours, salt and baking powder into a large bowl. Rub in the butter until the mixture resembles fine breadcrumbs.

2. Stir 4 tablespoons of the milk into the mashed potato and season with black pepper.

3. Add the dry ingredients to the potato mixture, mixing together with a fork and adding the remaining 1 tablespoon of milk if needed.

4. Knead the dough on a lightly floured surface for a few seconds until smooth. Roll out to a 15 cm/6 inch round and transfer to an oiled baking sheet. Mark the scone round into six wedges, cutting about halfway through with a small sharp knife.

5. Brush with milk, then sprinkle with the cheese and a faint dusting of paprika. Bake on the middle shelf of the preheated oven for 15 minutes, or until well risen and golden brown.

6. Transfer to a wire rack and leave to cool for 5 minutes before breaking into wedges. Serve warm or leave to cool completely. Once cool store the scones in an airtight tin. Garnish with a sprig of basil and serve split and buttered.

Ingredients   MAKES 6

200 g/7 oz self-raising flour
25 g/1 oz wholemeal flour
½ tsp salt
1½ tsp baking powder
25 g/1 oz butter, cubed
5 tbsp milk
175 g/6 oz cold mashed potato
freshly ground black pepper

To finish:

2 tbsp milk
40 g/1½ oz mature Cheddar cheese, finely grated
paprika pepper, to dust
sprig of basil, to garnish

Food fact

The scone supposedly acquired its name from the Stone of Destiny (or Scone) in Scotland where Scottish Kings were once crowned.

Moist Mincemeat Tea Loaf

1 Preheat the oven to 180°C/350°F/Gas Mark 4, 10 minutes before cooking. Oil and line the base of a 900 g/2 lb loaf tin with non-stick baking paper.

2 Sift the flour and mixed spice into a large bowl. Add the butter and rub in until the mixture resembles breadcrumbs.

3 Reserve 2 tablespoons of the flaked almonds and stir in the rest with the glacé cherries and sugar.

4 Make a well in the centre of the dry ingredients. Lightly whisk the eggs, then stir in the mincemeat, lemon zest and brandy or milk.

5 Add the egg mixture and fold together until blended. Spoon into the prepared loaf tin, smooth the top with the back of a spoon, then sprinkle over the reserved flaked almonds.

6 Bake on the middle shelf of the preheated oven for 30 minutes. Cover with foil to prevent the almonds browning too much. Bake for a further 30 minutes, or until well risen and a skewer inserted into the centre comes out clean.

7 Leave the tea loaf in the tin for 10 minutes before removing and cooling on a wire rack. Remove the lining paper, slice thickly and serve.

Ingredients   CUTS INTO 12 SLICES

225 g/8 oz self-raising flour
$\frac{1}{2}$ tsp ground mixed spice
125 g/4 oz cold butter, cubed
75 g/3 oz flaked almonds
25 g/1 oz glacé cherries, rinsed, dried and quartered
75 g/3 oz light muscovado sugar
2 medium eggs
250 g/9 oz prepared mincemeat
1 tsp lemon zest
2 tsp brandy or milk

Fruity Apple Tea Bread

1 Preheat the oven to 180°C/350°F/Gas Mark 4. Oil and line the base of a 900 g/2 lb loaf tin with non-stick baking paper.

2 Put the butter, sugar, sultanas and apple juice in a small saucepan. Heat gently, stirring occasionally, until the butter has melted. Tip into a bowl and leave to cool.

3 Stir in the chopped apple and beaten eggs. Sift the flour, spices and bicarbonate of soda over the apple mixture. Stir well, spoon into the prepared loaf tin and smooth the top level with the back of a spoon.

4 Toss the apple slices in lemon juice and arrange on top.

5 Bake in the preheated oven for 50 minutes. Cover with foil to prevent the top from browning too much.

6 Leave in the tin for 10 minutes before turning out to cool on to a wire rack.

7 Brush the top with golden syrup and leave to cool. Remove the lining paper, cut into thick slices and serve with curls of butter.

Ingredients   12 SLICES

125 g/4 oz butter
125 g/4 oz soft light brown sugar
275 g/10 oz sultanas
150 ml/¼ pint apple juice
1 eating apple, peeled, cored and
　　chopped
2 medium eggs, beaten
275 g/10 oz plain flour
½ tsp ground cinnamon
½ tsp ground ginger
2 tsp bicarbonate of soda
curls of butter, to serve

To decorate:

1 eating apple, cored and sliced
1 tsp lemon juice
1 tbsp golden syrup, warmed

Tasty tip

For an alcoholic version of this cake, soak the sultanas in brandy overnight before adding in step 2. To make the tea bread more moist in texture, add 1 grated carrot at the same time as the chopped apple in step 3.

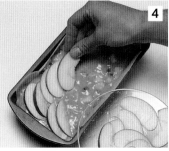

Baked Puddings & Sweet Tarts

The scrumptious tarts, pies and puddings in this section are great for sharing with friends and family, and some may take you back to your childhood days. Impress and indulge your guests with the Lattice Treacle Tart, Crunchy Rhubarb Crumble or heart-warming Jam Roly Poly. Don't forget to save yourself a slice!

Baked Lemon & Sultana Cheesecake

1   Preheat the oven to 170°C/325°F/Gas Mark 3. Oil a 20.5 cm/8 inch loose-bottomed round cake tin with non-stick baking paper.

2   Beat 50 g/2 oz of the sugar and the butter together until light and creamy, then stir in the self-raising flour, baking powder and 1 egg. Mix lightly together until well blended. Spoon into the prepared tin and spread the mixture over the base. Separate the 4 remaining eggs and reserve.

3   Blend the cheese in a food processor until soft. Gradually add the egg yolks and sugar and blend until smooth. Turn into a bowl and stir in the rest of the flour, lemon rind and juice. Mix lightly before adding the crème fraîche and sultanas, stirring well.

4   Whisk the egg whites until stiff, fold into the cheese mixture and pour into the tin. Tap lightly on the surface to remove any air bubbles. Bake in the preheated oven for about 1 hour, or until golden and firm.

5   Cover lightly if browning too much. Switch the oven off and leave in the oven to cool for 2–3 hours.

6   Remove the cheesecake from the oven and when completely cold, remove from the tin. Sprinkle with the icing sugar, decorate with the blackcurrants or blueberries and mint leaves and serve.

Ingredients   MAKES 10 SLICES

275 g/10 oz caster sugar
50 g/2 oz butter
50 g/2 oz self-raising flour
$1/2$ level tsp baking powder
5 large eggs
450 g/1 lb cream cheese
40 g/$1^{1}/_{2}$ oz plain flour
grated rind of 1 lemon
3 tbsp fresh lemon juice
150 ml/$^{1}/_{4}$ pint crème fraîche
75 g/3 oz sultanas

To decorate:

1 tbsp icing sugar
fresh blackcurrants or blueberries
mint leaves

Crunchy Rhubarb Crumble

1 Preheat the oven to 180°C/350°F/Gas Mark 4. Place the flour in a large bowl and cut the butter into cubes. Add to the flour and rub in with the fingertips until the mixture looks like fine breadcrumbs, or blend for a few seconds in a food processor.

2 Stir in the rolled oats, demerara sugar, sesame seeds and cinnamon. Mix well and reserve.

3 Prepare the rhubarb by removing the thick ends of the stalks and cut diagonally into 2.5 cm/1 inch chunks. Wash thoroughly and pat dry with a clean tea towel. Place the rhubarb in a 1.1 litre/2 pint pie dish.

4 Sprinkle the caster sugar over the rhubarb and top with the reserved crumble mixture. Level the top of the crumble so that all the fruit is well covered and press down firmly. If liked, sprinkle the top with a little extra caster sugar.

5 Place on a baking sheet and bake in the preheated oven for 40–50 minutes, or until the fruit is soft and the topping is golden brown. Sprinkle the pudding with some more caster sugar and serve hot with custard or cream.

Ingredients   SERVES 6

125 g/4 oz plain flour
50 g/2 oz softened butter
50 g/2 oz rolled oats
50 g/2 oz demerara sugar
1 tbsp sesame seeds
$1/2$ tsp ground cinnamon
450 g/1 lb fresh rhubarb
50 g/2 oz caster sugar
custard or cream, to serve

Tasty tip

To make homemade custard, pour 600 ml/1 pint of milk with a few drops of vanilla essence into a saucepan and bring to the boil. Remove from the heat and allow to cool. Meanwhile, whisk 5 egg yolks and 3 tablespoons of caster sugar together in a mixing bowl until thick and pale in colour. Add the milk, stir and strain into a heavy-based saucepan. Cook the custard on a low heat, stirring constantly until the consistency of double cream. Pour over the rhubarb crumble and serve.

Iced Bakewell Tart

1 Preheat the oven to 200°C/400°F/Gas Mark 6. Place the flour and salt in a bowl, rub in the butter and vegetable fat until the mixture resembles breadcrumbs. Alternatively, blend quickly, in short bursts, in a food processor.

2 Add the eggs with sufficient water to make a soft, pliable dough. Knead lightly on a floured board then chill in the refrigerator for about 30 minutes. Roll out the pastry and use to line a 23 cm/9 inch loose-bottomed flan tin.

3 For the filling, mix together the melted butter, sugar, almonds and beaten eggs and add a few drops of almond essence. Spread the base of the pastry case with the raspberry jam and spoon over the egg mixture.

4 Bake in the preheated oven for about 30 minutes, or until the filling is firm and golden brown. Remove from the oven and allow to cool completely.

5 When the tart is cold, make the icing by mixing together the icing sugar and lemon juice, a little at a time, until the icing is smooth and of a spreadable consistency.

6 Spread the icing over the tart, leave to set for 2–3 minutes and sprinkle with the almonds. Chill in the refrigerator for about 10 minutes and serve.

Ingredients   8 SLICES

For the rich pastry:

175 g/6 oz plain flour
pinch of salt
60 g/2½ oz butter, cut into
    small pieces
50 g/2 oz white vegetable fat,
    cut into small pieces
2 small egg yolks, beaten

For the filling:

125 g/4 oz butter, melted
125 g/4 oz caster sugar
125 g/4 oz ground almonds
2 large eggs, beaten
few drops of almond essence
2 tbsp seedless raspberry jam

For the icing:

125 g/4 oz icing sugar, sifted
6–8 tsp fresh lemon juice
25 g/1 oz toasted flaked almonds

Apricot & Almond Slice

1 Preheat the oven to 180°C/350°F/Gas Mark 4. Oil a 20.5 cm/8 inch square tin and line with non-stick baking paper.

2 Sprinkle the sugar and the flaked almonds over the paper, then arrange the apricot halves cut-side down on top.

3 Cream the butter and sugar together in a large bowl until light and fluffy.

4 Gradually beat the eggs into the butter mixture, adding a spoonful of flour after each addition of egg.

5 When all the eggs have been added, stir in the remaining flour and ground almonds and mix thoroughly.

6 Add the almond essence and the apricots and stir well.

7 Spoon the mixture into the prepared tin, taking care not to dislodge the apricot halves. Bake in the preheated oven for 1 hour, or until golden and firm to the touch.

8 Remove from the oven and allow to cool slightly for 15–20 minutes. Turn out carefully, discard the lining paper and transfer to a serving dish. Pour the honey over the top of the cake, sprinkle on the toasted almonds and serve.

Ingredients

MAKES 10 SLICES

2 tbsp demerara sugar
25 g/1 oz flaked almonds
400 g can apricot halves, drained
225 g/8 oz butter
225 g/8 oz caster sugar
4 medium eggs
200 g/7 oz self-raising flour
25 g/1 oz ground almonds
1/2 tsp almond essence
50 g/2 oz ready-to-eat dried
  apricots, chopped
3 tbsp clear honey
3 tbsp roughly chopped
  almonds, toasted

Helpful hint

This cake should keep for about three to five days if stored correctly. Allow the cake to cool completely, then remove from the tin and discard the lining paper. Store in an airtight container lined with greaseproof paper or baking parchment and keep in a cool place.

Queen of Puddings

1 Preheat the oven to 170°C/325°F/Gas Mark 3. Oil a 900 ml/1¹/₂ pint ovenproof baking dish and reserve.

2 Mix the breadcrumbs and sugar together in a bowl.

3 Pour the milk into a small saucepan and heat gently with the butter and lemon rind until the butter has melted. Allow the mixture to cool a little, then pour over the breadcrumbs. Stir well and leave to soak for 30 minutes.

4 Whisk the egg yolks into the cooled breadcrumb mixture and pour into the prepared dish.

5 Place the dish on a baking sheet and bake in the preheated oven for about 30 minutes, or until firm and set. Remove from the oven.

6 Allow to cool slightly, then spread the jam over the pudding. Whisk the egg whites until stiff and standing in peaks.

7 Gently fold in the caster sugar with a metal spoon or rubber spatula. Pile the meringue over the top of the pudding.

8 Return the dish to the oven for a further 25–30 minutes, or until the meringue is crisp and just slightly coloured. Serve hot or cold.

Ingredients   SERVES 4

75 g/3 oz fresh white breadcrumbs
25 g/1 oz granulated sugar
450 ml/³/₄ pint full-cream milk
25 g/1 oz butter
grated rind of 1 small lemon
2 medium eggs, separated
2 tbsp seedless raspberry jam
50 g/2 oz caster sugar

Helpful hint

When whisking egg whites it is imperative that the bowl is completely clean and free of any grease. To ensure that the meringue does not collapse, whisk the egg whites until stiff. Gradually add the sugar, a spoonful at a time, whisking well between each addition. Place in the oven immediately after all of the sugar has been added.

Crème Brûlée with Sugared Raspberries

1 Preheat the oven to 150°C/300°F/Gas Mark 2. Pour the cream into a bowl and place over a saucepan of gently simmering water. Heat gently but do not allow to boil.

2 Meanwhile, whisk together the egg yolks, 50 g/2 oz of the caster sugar and the vanilla essence. When the cream is warm, pour it over the egg mixture, whisking briskly until it is mixed completely.

3 Pour into six individual ramekin dishes and place in a roasting tin. Fill the tin with sufficient water to come halfway up the sides of the dishes. Bake in the preheated oven for about 1 hour, or until set. To test if set, carefully insert a round bladed knife into the centre – if the knife comes out clean they are set.

4 Remove the puddings from the roasting tin and allow to cool. Chill in the refrigerator, preferably overnight.

5 Sprinkle the sugar over the top of each dish and place the puddings under a preheated hot grill. When the sugar has caramelised and turned deep brown, remove from the heat and cool. Chill the puddings in the refrigerator for 2–3 hours before serving.

6 Toss the raspberries in the remaining caster sugar and sprinkle over the top of each dish. Serve with a little extra cream if liked.

Ingredients   SERVES 6

600 ml/1 pint fresh whipping cream
4 medium egg yolks
75 g/3 oz caster sugar
$^{1}/_{2}$ tsp vanilla essence
25 g/1 oz demerara sugar
175 g/6 oz fresh raspberries

Helpful hint

Most chefs use blow torches to brown the sugar in step 5, as this is the quickest way to caramelise the top of the dessert. Take great care if using a blow torch, especially when lighting. Otherwise use the grill, making sure that it is very hot and the dessert is thoroughly chilled before caramelising the sugar topping. This will prevent the custard underneath from melting.

Chocolate Sponge Pudding with Fudge Sauce

1 Preheat the oven to 170°C/325°F/Gas Mark 3. Oil a 900 ml/1¹/₂ pint pie dish.

2 Cream the butter and the sugar together in a large bowl until light and fluffy.

3 Stir in the melted chocolate, flour, drinking chocolate and egg and mix together.

4 Turn the mixture into the prepared dish and level the surface.

5 To make the fudge sauce, blend the brown sugar, cocoa powder and pecan nuts together and sprinkle evenly over the top of the pudding.

6 Stir the caster sugar into the hot black coffee until it has dissolved.

7 Carefully pour the coffee over the top of the pudding.

8 Bake in the preheated oven for 50–60 minutes, until the top is firm to touch. There will now be a rich sauce underneath the sponge.

9 Remove from the oven, dust with icing sugar and serve hot with crème fraîche.

Ingredients   SERVES 4

75 g/3 oz butter
75 g/3 oz caster sugar
50 g/2 oz plain dark chocolate, melted
50 g/2 oz self-raising flour
25 g/1 oz drinking chocolate
1 large egg
1 tbsp icing sugar, to dust
crème fraîche, to serve

For the fudge sauce:

50 g/2 oz soft light brown sugar
1 tbsp cocoa powder
40 g/1¹/₂ oz pecan nuts, roughly chopped
25 g/1 oz caster sugar
300 ml/¹/₂ pint hot, strong black coffee

Tasty tip

Try placing six halved and stoned fresh red plums in the base of the dish before adding the prepared chocolate sponge.

3

5

7

Lemon & Apricot Pudding

1 Preheat the oven to 180°C/350°F/Gas Mark 4. Oil a 1.1 litre/2 pint pie dish.

2 Soak the apricots in the orange juice for 10–15 minutes or until most of the juice has been absorbed, then place in the base of the pie dish.

3 Cream the butter and sugar together with the lemon rind until light and fluffy.

4 Separate the eggs. Beat the egg yolks into the creamed mixture with a spoonful of flour after each addition. Add the remaining flour and beat well until smooth.

5 Stir the milk and lemon juice into the creamed mixture. Whisk the egg whites in a grease-free mixing bowl until stiff and standing in peaks. Fold into the mixture using a metal spoon or rubber spatula.

6 Pour into the prepared dish and place in a baking tray filled with enough cold water to come halfway up the sides of the dish.

7 Bake in the preheated oven for about 45 minutes, or until the sponge is firm and golden brown. Remove from the oven. Serve immediately with the custard or fresh cream.

Ingredients   SERVES 4

125 g/4 oz ready-to-eat
  dried apricots
3 tbsp orange juice, warmed
50 g/2 oz butter
125 g/4 oz caster sugar
juice and grated rind of 2 lemons
2 medium eggs
100 g/4 oz self-raising flour
300 ml/$^1/_2$ pint milk
custard or fresh cream, to serve

Helpful hint

This pudding is cooked in a bain-marie to control the temperature around the dish – it needs to stay at just below boiling point. Bain-maries are ideal when cooking custards, sauces and other egg dishes. When using one, ensure that the water is kept topped up.

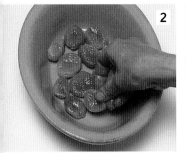

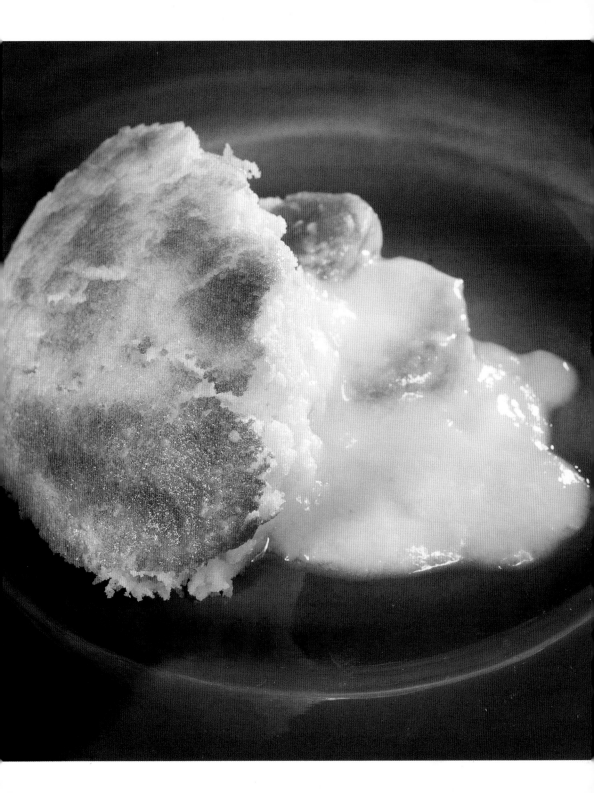

Strawberry Flan

1   Preheat the oven to 200°C/400°F/Gas Mark 6. Place the flour, butter and vegetable fat in a food processor and blend until the mixture resembles fine breadcrumbs. Stir in the sugar, then, with the machine running, add the egg yolk and enough water to make a fairly stiff dough. Knead lightly, cover and chill in the refrigerator for 30 minutes.

2   Roll out the pastry and use to line a 23 cm/9 inch loose-bottomed flan tin. Place a piece of greaseproof paper in the pastry case and cover with baking beans or rice. Bake in the preheated oven for 15–20 minutes, until just firm. Reserve until cool.

3   Make the filling by whisking the eggs and sugar together until thick and pale. Gradually stir in the flour and then the milk. Pour into a small saucepan and simmer for 3–4 minutes, stirring throughout.

4   Add the vanilla essence to taste, then pour into a bowl and leave to cool. Cover with greaseproof paper to prevent a skin from forming.

5   When the filling is cold, whisk until smooth then pour on to the cooked flan case. Slice the strawberries and arrange on the top of the filling. Decorate with the mint leaves and serve.

Ingredients   SERVES 6

Sweet pastry:

175 g/6 oz plain flour
50 g/2 oz butter
50 g/2 oz white vegetable fat
2 tsp caster sugar
1 medium egg yolk, beaten

For the filling:

1 medium egg, plus 1 extra egg yolk
50 g/2 oz caster sugar
25 g/1 oz plain flour
300 ml/$\frac{1}{2}$ pint milk
few drops of vanilla essence
450 g/1 lb strawberries,
   cleaned and hulled
mint leaves, to decorate

Rich Double-crust Plum Pie

1 Preheat the oven to 200°C/400°F/Gas Mark 6. Make the pastry by rubbing the butter and white vegetable fat into the flour until it resembles fine breadcrumbs or blend in a food processor. Add the egg yolks and enough water to make a soft dough. Knead lightly, then wrap and leave in the refrigerator for about 30 minutes.

2 Meanwhile, prepare the fruit. Rinse and dry the plums, then cut in half and remove the stones. Slice into chunks and cook in a saucepan with 25 g/1 oz of the sugar and 2 tablespoons of water for 5–7 minutes, or until slightly softened. Remove from the heat and add the remaining sugar to taste and allow to cool.

3 Roll out half the chilled pastry on a lightly floured surface and use to line the base and sides of a 1.1 litre/2 pint pie dish. Allow the pastry to hang over the edge. Spoon in the plums and brush the edge with a little water.

4 Roll out the remaining pastry to use as the lid. Wrap the pastry around the rolling pin and place over the plums. Press the edges together to seal and mark a decorative edge around the rim by pinching with the thumb and forefinger or using the back of a fork. Brush the lid with milk, and make a few slits in the top. Use any trimmings to decorate the pie with pastry leaves. Place on a baking sheet and bake in the preheated oven for 30 minutes, or until golden brown. Sprinkle with a little caster sugar and serve hot or cold.

Ingredients SERVES 6

For the pastry:
75 g/3 oz butter
75 g/3 oz white vegetable fat
225 g/8 oz plain flour
2 medium egg yolks

For the filling:
450 g/1 lb fresh plums,
   preferably Victoria
50 g/2 oz caster sugar
1 tbsp milk
a little extra caster sugar

Helpful hint
As Victoria plums have only a short season, from August to September, you can also use other varieties that have been imported. Alternatively buy English plums in season. Halve, store and freeze them, then use as required.

Baked Apple Dumplings

1 Preheat the oven to 200°C/400°F/Gas Mark 6. Lightly oil a baking tray. Place the flour and salt in a bowl and stir in the suet. Add just enough water to the mixture to mix to a soft, but not sticky, dough, using the fingertips.

2 Turn the dough on to a lightly floured board and knead lightly into a ball. Divide the dough into four pieces and roll out each piece into a thin square, large enough to encase the apples.

3 Peel and core the apples and place 1 apple in the centre of each square of pastry.

4 Fill the centre of the apple with mincemeat, brush the edges of each pastry square with water and draw the corners up to meet over each apple.

5 Press the edges of the pastry firmly together and decorate with pastry leaves and shapes made from the extra pastry trimmings.

6 Place the apples on the prepared baking tray, brush with the egg white and sprinkle with the sugar.

7 Bake in the preheated oven for 30 minutes, or until golden and the pastry and apples are cooked. Serve the dumplings hot with the custard or vanilla sauce.

Ingredients   SERVES 4

225 g/8 oz self-raising flour
$1/4$ tsp salt
125 g/4 oz shredded suet
4 medium cooking apples
4–6 tsp luxury mincemeat
1 medium egg white, beaten
2 tsp caster sugar
custard or vanilla sauce, to serve

Tasty tip

To make vanilla sauce, blend $1^{1}/_{2}$ tablespoons of cornflour with 3 tablespoons of milk to a smooth paste. Bring just under 300 ml/$^{1}/_{2}$ pint of milk to just below boiling point. Stir in the cornflour paste and cook over a gentle heat, stirring throughout until thickened and smooth. Remove from the heat and add 1 tablespoon of caster sugar, a knob of butter and $1/2$ teaspoon of vanilla essence. Stir until the sugar and butter have melted, then serve.

1

4

5

Jam Roly Poly

1 Preheat the oven to 200°C/400°F/Gas Mark 6. Make the pastry by sifting the flour and salt into a large bowl. Add the suet and mix lightly, then add the water a little at a time and mix to form a soft and pliable dough. Take care not to make the dough too wet. Turn the dough out on to a lightly floured board and knead gently until smooth. Roll the dough out into a 23 x 28 cm/9 x 11 inch rectangle.

2 Spread the jam over the pastry leaving a border of 1 cm/^{1}/$_2$ inch all round. Fold the border over the jam and brush the edges with water.

3 Lightly roll the rectangle up from one of the short sides, seal the top edge and press the ends together. Do not roll the pudding up too tightly.

4 Turn the pudding upside down on to a piece of greaseproof paper large enough to come halfway up the sides. If using non-stick paper, then oil lightly. Tie the ends of the paper, to make a boat-shaped paper case for the pudding to sit in and to leave plenty of room for the roly poly to expand. Brush the pudding lightly with milk and sprinkle with the sugar. Bake in the preheated oven for 30–40 minutes, or until well risen and golden. Serve immediately with the jam sauce.

Ingredients   SERVES 6

225 g/8 oz self-raising flour
^{1}/$_4$ tsp salt
125 g/4 oz shredded suet
about 150 ml/^{1}/$_4$ pint water
3 tbsp strawberry jam
1 tbsp milk, to glaze
1 tsp caster sugar
ready-made jam sauce, to serve

Tasty tip

To make jam sauce, warm 4 tablespoons of jam such as seedless raspberry jam with 150 ml/^{1}/$_4$ pint of water or orange juice. Stir until smooth. Blend 2 teaspoons of arrowroot with 1 tablespoon of water or juice to a smooth paste. Bring the jam mixture to almost boiling point, then stir in the blended arrowroot. Cook, stirring until the mixture thickens slightly and clears, then serve.

Egg Custard Tart

1 Preheat the oven to 200°C/400°F/Gas Mark 6. Oil a 20.5 cm/8 inch flan tin or dish.

2 Make the pastry by cutting the butter and vegetable fat into small cubes, then add to the flour in a large bowl and rub in, until the mixture resembles fine breadcrumbs.

3 Add the egg, sugar and enough water to form a soft and pliable dough. Turn on to a lightly floured board and knead. Wrap and chill in the refrigerator for 30 minutes.

4 Roll the pastry out on to a lightly floured surface or pastry board and use to line the oiled flan tin. Place in the refrigerator and reserve.

5 Warm the milk in a small saucepan. Briskly whisk together the eggs, egg yolk and caster sugar.

6 Pour the milk into the egg mixture and whisk until blended. Strain through a sieve into the pastry case. Place the flan tin on a baking sheet. Sprinkle the top of the tart with nutmeg and bake in the preheated oven for about 15 minutes.

7 Turn the oven down to 170°C/325°F/Gas Mark 3 and bake for a further 30 minutes, or until the custard has set. Serve hot or cold.

Ingredients   SERVES 6
Sweet pastry:
50 g/2 oz butter
50 g/2 oz white vegetable fat
175 g/6 oz plain flour
1 medium egg yolk, beaten
2 tsp caster sugar

For the filling:
300 ml/½ pint milk
2 medium eggs, plus 1 medium
   egg yolk
25 g/1 oz caster sugar
½ tsp freshly grated nutmeg

Helpful hint
Nowadays eggs are normally date stamped so it is possible to ensure that they are eaten when they are at their best. Another way to test if an egg is fresh is to place an uncooked egg in a bowl of water – if it lies at the bottom it is fresh; if it tilts it is older (use for frying or scrambling); if it floats, discard.

Golden Castle Pudding

1 Preheat the oven to 180°C/350°F/Gas Mark 4. Lightly oil 4–6 individual pudding bowls and place a small circle of lightly oiled non-stick baking or greaseproof paper in the base of each one.

2 Place the butter and caster sugar in a large bowl, then beat together until the mixture is pale and creamy. Stir in the vanilla essence and gradually add the beaten eggs, a little at a time. Add a tablespoon of flour after each addition of egg and beat well.

3 When the mixture is smooth, add the remaining flour and fold in gently. Add a tablespoon of water and mix to form a soft mixture that will drop easily off a spoon.

4 Spoon enough mixture into each basin to come halfway up the tin, allowing enough space for the puddings to rise. Place on a baking sheet and bake in the preheated oven for about 25 minutes until firm and golden brown.

5 Allow the puddings to stand for 5 minutes. Turn out on to individual serving plates and discard the paper circle.

6 Warm the golden syrup in a small saucepan and pour a little over each pudding. Serve hot with the crème fraîche or custard.

Ingredients   SERVES 4–6

125 g/4 oz butter
125 g/4 oz caster sugar
a few drops of vanilla essence
2 medium eggs, beaten
125 g/4 oz self-raising flour
4 tbsp golden syrup
crème fraîche or ready-made
   custard, to serve

Cherry Batter Pudding

1 Preheat the oven to 220°C/425°F/Gas Mark 7. Lightly oil a 900 ml/1½ pint shallow baking dish.

2 Rinse the cherries, drain well and remove the stones (using a cherry stoner if possible). If using canned cherries, drain well and discard the juice. Place in the prepared dish.

3 Sift the flour and salt into a large bowl. Stir in 2 tablespoons of the caster sugar and make a well in the centre. Beat the eggs, then pour into the well of the dry ingredients.

4 Warm the milk and slowly pour into the well, beating throughout and gradually drawing in the flour from the sides of the bowl. Continue until a smooth batter has formed.

5 Melt the butter in a small saucepan over a low heat, then stir into the batter with the rum. Reserve for 15 minutes, then beat again until smooth and easy to pour.

6 Pour into the prepared baking dish and bake in the preheated oven for 30–35 minutes, or until golden brown and set.

7 Remove the pudding from the oven, sprinkle with the remaining sugar and serve hot with plenty of fresh cream.

Ingredients   SERVES 4

450 g/1 lb fresh cherries (or 425 g
  can pitted cherries)
50 g/2 oz plain flour
pinch of salt
3 tbsp caster sugar
2 medium eggs
300 ml/½ pint milk
40 g/1½ oz butter
1 tbsp rum
extra caster sugar, to dust
fresh cream, to serve

Food fact

The traditional name of this French speciality is *clafoutis*. For that extra hit of cherry flavour why not replace the rum used in this recipe with kirsch – an eau-de-vie rather than a liqueur which is made from pine kernels and cherry fruit juice to produce a brandy. It is made in Alsace as well as in the Blackforest region in Germany.

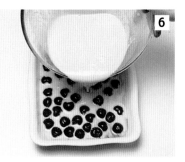

Apple & Cinnamon Brown Betty

1 Preheat the oven to 180°C/350°F/Gas Mark 4. Lightly oil a 900 ml/1½ pint ovenproof dish. Peel, core and slice the apples and place in a saucepan with the caster sugar, lemon rind and 2 tablespoons of water. Simmer for 10–15 minutes or until tender.

2 Mix the breadcrumbs with the sugar and the cinnamon. Place half the sweetened apples in the base of the prepared dish and spoon over half of the crumb mixture. Place the remaining apples on top and cover with the rest of the crumb mixture.

3 Melt the butter and pour over the surface of the pudding. Cover the dish with non-stick baking paper and bake in the preheated oven for 20 minutes. Remove the paper and bake for a further 10–15 minutes, or until golden.

4 Meanwhile, make the custard by whisking the egg yolks and sugar together until creamy. Mix 1 tablespoon of the milk with the cornflour until a paste forms and reserve.

5 Warm the rest of the milk until nearly boiling and pour over the egg mixture with the paste and vanilla essence.

6 Place the bowl over a saucepan of gently simmering water. Stir over the heat until the custard is thickened and can coat the back of a spoon. Strain into a jug and serve hot over the pudding.

Ingredients   SERVES 4

450 g/1 lb cooking apples
50 g/2 oz caster sugar
finely grated rind of 1 lemon
125 g/4 oz fresh white breadcrumbs
125 g/4 oz demerara sugar
½ tsp ground cinnamon
25 g/1 oz butter

For the custard:

3 medium egg yolks
1 tbsp caster sugar
500 ml/1 pint milk
1 tbsp cornflour
few drops of vanilla essence

Tasty tip

For a richer, more luxurious custard, substitute the milk in this recipe for double cream and increase the number of eggs yolks used to 4.

Lattice Treacle Tart

1 Preheat the oven to 190°C/375°F/Gas Mark 5. Make the pastry by placing the flour, butter and white vegetable fat in a food processor. Blend in short sharp bursts until the mixture resembles fine breadcrumbs. Remove from the processor and place on a pastry board or in a large bowl.

2 Stir in enough cold water to make a dough and knead in a large bowl or on a floured surface until smooth and pliable.

3 Roll out the pastry and use to line a 20.5 cm/ 8 inch loose-bottomed fluted flan dish or tin. Reserve the pastry trimmings for decoration. Chill for 30 minutes.

4 Meanwhile, to make the filling, place the golden syrup in a saucepan and warm gently with the lemon rind and juice. Tip the breadcrumbs into the pastry case and pour the syrup mixture over the top.

5 Roll the pastry trimmings out on a lightly floured surface and cut into 6–8 thin strips. Lightly dampen the pastry edge of the tart, then place the strips across the filling in a lattice pattern. Brush the ends of the strips with water and seal to the edge of the tart. Brush a little beaten egg over the pastry and bake in the preheated oven for 25 minutes, or until the filling is just set. Serve hot or cold.

Ingredients   SERVES 4

For the pastry:
175 g/6 oz plain flour
40 g/1½ oz butter
40 g/1½ oz white vegetable fat

For the filling:
225 g/8 oz golden syrup
juice and finely grated rind
   of 1 lemon
75 g/3 oz fresh white breadcrumbs
1 small egg, beaten

Tasty tip
A tasty alternative can be made by replacing the breadcrumbs with the same amount of dessicated coconut.

Everyday Cakes

This section contains recipes for those classic cakes and buns that always spring to mind. Often we do not have the time or inclination to make a fancy cake and just want to whip up a simple but delicious and traditional treat. You are sure to have a hit with everything here, including Lemon Drizzle Cake, Fruit Cake and Coffee & Pecan Cake.

Lemon & Ginger Buns

1 Preheat the oven to 220°C/425°F/Gas Mark 7, 15 minutes before baking. Cut the butter or margarine into small pieces and place in a large bowl.

2 Sift the flour, baking powder, ginger and salt together and add to the butter with the lemon rind.

3 Using the fingertips, rub the butter into the flour and spice mixture until it resembles coarse breadcrumbs.

4 Stir in the sugar, sultanas, chopped mixed peel and stem ginger.

5 Add the egg and lemon juice to the mixture, then, using a round-bladed knife, stir well to mix. The mixture should be quite stiff and just holding together.

6 Place heaped tablespoons of the mixture on to a lightly oiled baking tray, making sure that the dollops of mixture are well apart.

7 Using a fork, rough up the edges of the buns and bake in the preheated oven for 12–15 minutes.

8 Leave the buns to cool for 5 minutes before transferring to a wire rack until cold, then serve. Otherwise store the buns in an airtight container and eat within 3–5 days.

Ingredients   MAKES 15

175 g/6 oz butter or margarine
350 g/12 oz plain flour
2 tsp baking powder
$1/2$ tsp ground ginger
pinch of salt
finely grated rind of 1 lemon
175 g/6 oz soft light brown sugar
125 g/4 oz sultanas
75 g/3 oz chopped mixed peel
25 g/1 oz stem ginger,
    finely chopped
1 medium egg
juice of 1 lemon

Tasty tip

For a gooey, sticky treat, brush the buns with a little syrup from the jar of stem ginger, and scatter with some extra finely chopped stem ginger as soon as they have been removed from the oven.

Apple & Cinnamon Crumble-top Cake

1 Preheat the oven to 180°C/350°F/Gas Mark 4, 10 minutes before baking. Lightly oil and line the base of a 20.5 cm/8 inch deep round cake tin with greaseproof or baking paper.

2 Finely chop the apples and mix with the lemon juice. Reserve while making the cake.

3 For the crumble topping, sift the flour and cinnamon together into a large bowl.

4 Rub the butter or margarine into the flour and cinnamon until the mixture resembles coarse breadcrumbs.

5 Stir the sugar into the butter and flour mixture and reserve.

6 For the base, cream the butter or margarine and sugar together until light and fluffy. Gradually beat the eggs in a little at a time until all the egg has been added.

7 Sift flour and gently fold in with a metal spoon or rubber spatula.

8 Spoon into the base of the prepared cake tin. Arrange the apple pieces on top, then lightly stir the milk into the crumble mixture.

9 Scatter the crumble mixture over the apples and bake in the preheated oven for 1½ hours. Serve cold with cream or custard.

Ingredients

CUTS INTO
8 SLICES

For the topping:
350 g/12 oz eating apples, peeled
1 tbsp lemon juice
125 g/4 oz self-raising flour
1 tsp ground cinnamon
75 g/3 oz butter or margarine
75 g/3 oz demerara sugar
1 tbsp milk

For the base:
125 g/4 oz butter or margarine
125 g/4 oz caster sugar
2 medium eggs
150 g/5 oz self-raising flour
cream or freshly made custard,
    to serve

Tasty tip
For a crunchier-textured topping, stir in 50 g/2 oz of chopped mixed nuts and seeds to the crumble mixture in step 5.

2

6

9

Chocolate & Coconut Cake

1 Preheat the oven to 180°C/350°F/Gas Mark 4, 10 minutes before baking. Melt the chocolate in a small bowl placed over a saucepan of gently simmering water, ensuring that the base of the bowl does not touch the water. When the chocolate has melted, stir until smooth and allow to cool.

2 Lightly oil and line the bases of two 18 cm/7 inch sandwich tins with greaseproof or baking paper. In a large bowl beat the butter or margarine and sugar together with a wooden spoon until light and creamy. Beat in the eggs a little at a time, then stir in the melted chocolate.

3 Sift the flour and cocoa powder together and gently fold into the chocolate mixture with a metal spoon or rubber spatula. Add the desiccated coconut and mix lightly. Divide between the two prepared tins and smooth the tops.

4 Bake in the preheated oven for 25–30 minutes, or until a skewer comes out clean when inserted into the centre of the cake. Allow to cool in the tin for 5 minutes, then turn out, discard the lining paper and leave on a wire rack until cold.

5 Beat together the butter or margarine and creamed coconut until light. Add the icing sugar and mix well. Spread half the icing on one cake and press the cakes together. Spread the remaining icing over the top, sprinkle with the coconut and serve.

Ingredients
CUTS INTO 8 SLICES

125 g/4 oz plain dark chocolate, roughly chopped
175 g/6 oz butter or margarine
175 g/6 oz caster sugar
3 medium eggs, beaten
175 g/6 oz self-raising flour
1 tbsp cocoa powder
50 g/2 oz desiccated coconut

For the icing:
125 g/4 oz butter or margarine
2 tbsp creamed coconut
225 g/8 oz icing sugar
25 g/1 oz desiccated coconut, lightly toasted

Tasty tip
Why not experiment with the chocolate in this recipe? For a different taste, try using orange-flavoured dark chocolate or add 1–2 tablespoons of rum when melting the chocolate.

Citrus Cake

1 Preheat the oven to 325°C/170°F/Gas Mark 3, 10 minutes before baking. Lightly oil and line the base of a round 20.5 cm/8 inch deep cake tin with baking paper.

2 In a large bowl, cream the sugar and butter or margarine together until light and fluffy. Whisk the eggs together and beat into the creamed mixture a little at a time.

3 Beat in the orange juice with 1 tablespoon of the flour. Sift the remaining flour on to a large plate several times, then, with a metal spoon or rubber spatula, fold into the creamed mixture.

4 Spoon into the prepared cake tin. Stir the finely grated orange rind into the lemon curd and dot randomly across the top of the mixture.

5 Using a fine skewer swirl the lemon curd through the cake mixture. Bake in the preheated oven for 35 minutes, until risen and golden. Allow to cool for 5 minutes in the tin, then turn out carefully on to a wire rack.

6 Sift the icing sugar into a bowl, add the grated lemon rind and juice and stir well to mix. When the cake is cold cover the top with the icing and serve.

Ingredients

CUTS INTO
6 SLICES

175 g/6 oz golden caster sugar
175 g/6 oz butter or margarine
3 medium eggs
2 tbsp orange juice
175 g/6 oz self-raising flour
finely grated rind of 2 oranges
5 tbsp lemon curd
125 g/4 oz icing sugar
finely grated rind of 1 lemon
1 tbsp freshly squeezed lemon juice

Food fact

Repeated sifting as in step 3 removes impurities from the flour while adding air to it. Using golden caster sugar gives a richer, sweeter taste than normal caster sugar and contrasts particularly well with the citrus flavours in this cake.

Victoria Sponge with Mango & Mascarpone

1. Preheat the oven to 190°C/375°F/Gas Mark 5, 10 minutes before baking. Lightly oil two 18 cm/7 inch sandwich tins and dust lightly with caster sugar and flour, tapping the tins to remove any excess.

2. In a large bowl cream the butter or margarine and sugar together with a wooden spoon until light and creamy. In another bowl mix the eggs and vanilla essence together. Sift the flour several times on to a plate. Beat a little egg into the butter and sugar, then a little flour and beat well.

3. Continue adding the flour and eggs alternately, beating between each addition, until the mixture is well mixed and smooth. Divide the mixture between the two prepared cake tins, level the surface, then, using the back of a large spoon, make a slight dip in the centre of each cake.

4. Bake in the preheated oven for 25–30 minutes, until the centre of the cake springs, back, when gently pressed with a clean finger. Turn out on to a wire rack and leave the cakes until cold.

5. Beat the icing sugar and mascarpone cheese together, then chop the mango into small cubes. Use half the mascarpone and mango to sandwich the cakes together. Spread the rest of the mascarpone on top, decorate with the remaining mango and serve. To store, cover lightly and refrigerate. Use within 3–4 days.

Ingredients
CUTS INTO 8 SLICES

175 g/6 oz caster sugar, plus extra for dusting
175 g/6 oz self-raising flour, plus extra for dusting
175 g/6 oz butter or margarine
3 large eggs
1 tsp vanilla essence
25 g/1 oz icing sugar
250 g/9 oz mascarpone cheese
1 large ripe mango, peeled

Tasty tip
Mango has been used in this recipe, but 125 g/4 oz of mashed strawberries could be used instead. Reserve a few whole strawberries, slice and use to decorate the cake.

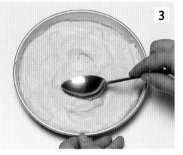
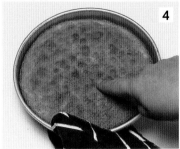

Almond Cake

1. Preheat the oven to 150°C/300°F/Gas Mark 2. Lightly oil and line the base of a 20.5 cm/8 inch deep round cake tin with greaseproof or baking paper.

2. Cream together the butter or margarine and sugar with a wooden spoon until light and fluffy.

3. Beat the eggs and essences together. Gradually add to the sugar and butter mixture and mix well between each addition.

4. Sift the flour and mix with the ground almonds. Beat into the egg mixture until mixed well and smooth. Pour into the prepared cake tin.

5. Roughly chop the whole almonds and scatter over the cake. Bake in the preheated oven for 45 minutes, or until golden and risen and a skewer inserted into the centre of the cake comes out clean.

6. Remove from the tin and leave to cool on a wire rack. Melt the chocolate in a small bowl placed over a saucepan of gently simmering water, stirring until smooth and free of lumps.

7. Drizzle the melted chocolate over the cooled cake and serve once the chocolate has set.

Ingredients
CUTS INTO 8 SLICES

225 g/8 oz butter or margarine
225 g/8 oz caster sugar
3 large eggs
1 tsp vanilla essence
1 tsp almond essence
125 g/4 oz self-raising flour
175 g/6 oz ground almonds
50 g/2 oz whole almonds, blanched
25 g/1 oz plain dark chocolate

Tasty tip

Baking with ground almonds helps to keep the cake moist as well as adding a slight nutty flavour to the cake. 1–2 tablespoons of orange water can be added with the zest of 1 orange in step 4 if a fragrant citrus flavour is desired, but do omit the vanilla essence.

2

5

7

Lemon Drizzle Cake

1 Preheat the oven to 180°C/350°F/Gas Mark 4, 10 minutes before baking. Lightly oil and line the base of an 18 cm/7 inch square cake tin with baking paper.

2 In a large bowl, cream the butter or margarine and sugar together until soft and fluffy. Beat the eggs, then gradually add a little of the egg to the creamed mixture, adding 1 tablespoon of flour after each addition.

3 Finely grate the rind from 1 of the lemons and stir into the creamed mixture, beating well until smooth. Squeeze the juice from the lemon, strain, then stir into the mixture. Spoon into the prepared tin, level the surface and bake in the preheated oven for 25–30 minutes.

4 Using a zester, remove the peel from the last lemon and mix with 25 g/1 oz of the granulated sugar and reserve. Squeeze the juice into a small saucepan. Add the rest of the granulated sugar to the lemon juice in the saucepan and heat gently, stirring occasionally. When the sugar has dissolved simmer gently for 3–4 minutes until syrupy.

5 With a cocktail stick or fine skewer prick the cake all over. Sprinkle the lemon zest and sugar over the top of the cake, drizzle over the syrup and leave to cool in the tin. Cut the cake into squares and serve.

Ingredients   CUTS INTO 16 SQUARES

125 g/4 oz butter or margarine
175 g/6 oz caster sugar
2 large eggs
175 g/6 oz self-raising flour
2 lemons, preferably unwaxed
50 g/2 oz granulated sugar

Food fact

This classic cake is a favourite in many kitchens. The buttery sponge is perfectly complemented by the lemon syrup, which soaks into the cake giving it a gooeyness which is even better the next day!

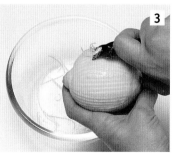

Double Chocolate Cake with Cinnamon

1 Preheat the oven to 190°C/375°F/Gas Mark 5, 10 minutes before baking. Lightly oil and line the base of two 20.5 cm/8 inch sandwich tins with greaseproof or baking paper. Sift the cocoa powder, cinnamon and flour together and reserve.

2 In a large bowl, cream the butter or margarine and sugar, until light and fluffy. Beat in the eggs a little at a time until they are all incorporated and the mixture is smooth. If it looks curdled at any point beat in 1 tablespoon of the sifted flour.

3 Using a rubber spatula or metal spoon, fold the sifted flour and cocoa powder into the egg mixture until well mixed .

4 Divide between the two prepared cake tins, and level the surface. Bake in the preheated oven for 25–30 minutes, until springy to the touch and a skewer inserted into the centre of the cake comes out clean. Turn out on to a wire rack to cool.

5 To make the filling, coarsely break the white chocolate and heat the cream very gently in a small saucepan. Add the broken chocolate, stirring until melted. Leave to cool, then using half the cooled white chocolate, sandwich the cakes together.

6 Top the cake with the remaining cooled white chocolate. Coarsely grate the dark chocolate over the top and serve.

Ingredients
CUTS INTO
10 SLICES

50 g/2 oz cocoa powder
1 tsp ground cinnamon
225 g/8 oz self-raising flour
225 g/8 oz unsalted butter
   or margarine
225 g/8 oz caster sugar
4 large eggs

For the filling:
125 g/4 oz white chocolate
50 ml/2 fl oz double cream
25 g/1 oz plain dark chocolate

Helpful hint
Adding some sifted flour can help to prevent the mixture from curdling (see step 2). Removing the eggs from the refrigerator and allowing them to return to room temperature before use also helps. Remember to add just a little egg at a time!

Swiss Roll

1 Preheat the oven to 220°C/425°F/Gas Mark 7, 15 minutes before baking. Lightly oil and line the base of a 23 x 33 cm/9 x 13 inch Swiss roll tin with a single sheet of greaseproof or baking paper.

2 Sift the flour several times, then reserve on top of the oven to warm a little. Place a mixing bowl with the eggs, vanilla essence and sugar over a saucepan of hot water, ensuring that the base of the bowl is not touching the water. With the saucepan off the heat whisk with an electric hand whisk until the egg mixture becomes pale and mousse-like and has increased in volume. Remove the basin from the saucepan and continue to whisk for a further 2–3 minutes. Sift in the flour and very gently fold in using a metal spoon or rubber spatula, trying not to knock out the air whisked in already. Pour into the prepared tin, tilting to ensure that the mixture is evenly distributed. Bake in the preheated oven for 10–12 minutes, or until well risen, golden brown and the top springs back when touched lightly with a clean finger.

3 Sprinkle the toasted, chopped hazelnuts over a large sheet of greaseproof paper. When the cake has cooked turn out on to the hazelnut covered paper and trim the edges of the cake. Holding an edge of the paper with the short side of the cake nearest you, roll the cake up. When fully cold carefully unroll and spread with the jam and then the cream. Roll back up and serve. Otherwise, store in the refrigerator and eat within 2 days.

Ingredients

CUTS INTO
8 SLICES

75 g/3 oz self-raising flour
3 large eggs
1 tsp vanilla essence
90 g/3¹/₂ oz caster sugar
25 g/1 oz hazelnuts, toasted and
  finely chopped
3 tbsp apricot conserve
300 ml/¹/₂ pint double cream,
  lightly whipped

Tasty tip

Any flavour of jam can be used in this recipe. While apricot jam is delicious, traditional raspberry or blackcurrant jam also works very well. In place of the cream why not try buttercream icing or beaten mascarpone as a filling?

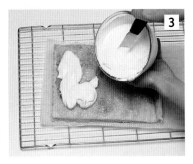

Toffee Apple Cake

1 Preheat the oven to 180°C/350°F/Gas Mark 4, 10 minutes before baking. Lightly oil and line the bases of two 20.5 cm/8 inch sandwich tins with greaseproof or baking paper.

2 Thinly slice the apples and toss in the brown sugar until well coated. Arrange them over the base of the prepared tins and reserve.

3 Cream together the butter or margarine and caster sugar until light and fluffy.

4 Beat the eggs together in a small bowl and gradually beat them into the creamed mixture, beating well between each addition.

5 Sift the flour into the mixture, and using a metal spoon or rubber spatula, fold in.

6 Divide the mixture between the two cake tins and level the surface. Bake in the preheated oven for 25–30 minutes, until golden and well risen. Leave in the tins to cool.

7 Lightly whip the cream with 1 tablespoon of the icing sugar and vanilla essence.

8 Sandwich the cakes together with the cream. Mix the remaining icing sugar and ground cinnamon together, sprinkle over the top of the cake and serve.

Ingredients   CUTS INTO 8 SLICES

2 small eating apples, peeled
4 tbsp soft dark brown sugar
175 g/6 oz butter or margarine
175 g/6 oz caster sugar
3 medium eggs
175 g/6 oz self-raising flour
150 ml/$^1/_4$ pint double cream
2 tbsp icing sugar
$^1/_2$ tsp vanilla essence
$^1/_2$ tsp ground cinnamon

Tasty tip

The dark brown sugar used in this recipe could be replaced with a dark muscovado sugar to give a deliciously rich toffee flavour to the apples. When baked, the sugar will melt slightly into a caramel consistency.

2

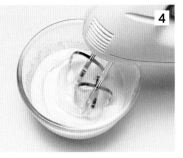

4

8

Cappuccino Cakes

1   Preheat the oven to 190°C/375°F/Gas Mark 5, 10 minutes before baking. Place six large paper muffin cases into a muffin tin or alternatively place on to a baking sheet.

2   Cream the butter or margarine and sugar together until light and fluffy. Break the eggs into a small bowl and beat lightly with a fork. Using a wooden spoon, beat the eggs into the butter and sugar mixture a little at a time, until they are all incorporated. If the mixture looks curdled, beat in a spoonful of the flour to return the mixture to a smooth consistency. Finally beat in the black coffee.

3   Sift the flour into the mixture, then, with a metal spoon or rubber spatula, gently fold in the flour.

4   Place spoonfuls of the mixture into the muffin cases. Bake in the preheated oven for 20–25 minutes, or until risen and springy to the touch. Cool on a wire rack.

5   In a small bowl beat together the mascarpone cheese, icing sugar and vanilla essence.

6   When the cakes are cold, spoon the vanilla mascarpone on to the top of each one. Dust with cocoa powder and serve. Eat within 24 hours and store in the refrigerator.

Ingredients   MAKES 6

125 g/4 oz butter or margarine
125 g/4 oz caster sugar
2 medium eggs
1 tbsp strong black coffee
150 g/5 oz self-raising flour
125 g/4 oz mascarpone cheese
1 tbsp icing sugar, sifted
1 tsp vanilla essence
sifted cocoa powder, to dust

Tasty tip

The combination of coffee with the vanilla-flavoured mascarpone is delicious. Make sure, however, that you use a good-quality coffee in this recipe. Colombian coffee is generally good and at its best possesses a smooth, rounded flavour.

Fruit Cake

1 Preheat the oven to 150°C/300°F/Gas Mark 2, 10 minutes before baking. Lightly oil and line a 23 cm/9 inch deep round cake tin with a double thickness of greaseproof paper.

2 In a large bowl, cream together the butter or margarine, sugar and orange rind until light and fluffy, then beat in the treacle.

3 Beat in the eggs a little at a time, beating well between each addition.

4 Reserve 1 tablespoon of the flour. Sift the remaining flour, the spices and bicarbonate of soda into the mixture.

5 Mix all the fruits and the reserved flour together, then stir into the cake mixture.

6 Turn into the prepared tin and smooth the top, making a small hollow in the centre of the cake mixture.

7 Bake in the preheated oven for 1 hour, then reduce the heat to 140°C/275°F/Gas Mark 1.

8 Bake for a further 1½ hours, or until cooked and a skewer inserted into the centre comes out clean. Leave to cool in the tin, then turn the cake out and serve. Otherwise, when cold store in an airtight tin.

Ingredients

CUTS INTO 10 SLICES

225 g/8 oz butter or margarine
200 g/7 oz soft brown sugar
finely grated rind of 1 orange
1 tbsp black treacle
3 large eggs, beaten
275 g/10 oz plain flour
¼ tsp ground cinnamon
½ tsp mixed spice
pinch of freshly grated nutmeg
¼ tsp bicarbonate of soda
75 g/3 oz mixed peel
50 g/2 oz glacé cherries
125 g/4 oz raisins
125 g/4 oz sultanas
125 g/4 oz ready-to-eat dried
  apricots, chopped

Tasty tip

For a fruit cake with a kick, when the cake has cooled, turn out and make holes in the base of the cake with a skewer. Dribble over 4–5 tablespoons of your favourite alcohol such as whisky, brandy or Drambuie.

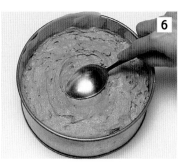

Banana Cake

1 Preheat the oven to 190°C/375°F/Gas Mark 5, 10 minutes before baking. Lightly oil and line the base of an 18 cm/7 inch deep round cake tin with greaseproof or baking paper.

2 Mash two of the bananas in a small bowl, sprinkle with the lemon juice and a heaped tablespoon of the sugar. Mix together lightly and reserve.

3 Gently heat the remaining sugar and butter or margarine in a small saucepan until the butter has just melted. Pour into a small bowl, then allow to cool slightly. Sift the flour and cinnamon into a large bowl and make a well in the centre.

4 Beat the eggs into the cooled sugar mixture, pour into the well of flour, and mix thoroughly.

5 Gently stir in the mashed banana mixture. Pour half of the mixture into the prepared tin. Thinly slice the remaining banana and arrange over the cake mixture. Sprinkle over the chopped walnuts, then cover with the remaining cake mixture.

6 Bake in the preheated oven for 50–55 minutes, or until well risen and golden brown. Allow to cool in the tin, turn out and sprinkle with the ground cinnamon and caster sugar. Serve hot or cold with a jug of fresh cream for pouring.

Ingredients CUTS INTO 8 SLICES

3 medium-sized ripe bananas
1 tsp lemon juice
150 g/5 oz soft brown sugar
75 g/3 oz butter or margarine
250 g/9 oz self-raising flour
1 tsp ground cinnamon
3 medium eggs
50 g/2 oz walnuts, chopped
1 tsp each ground cinnamon and
   caster sugar, to decorate
fresh cream, to serve

Helpful hint

The riper the bananas used in this recipe the better. Look out for reductions in supermarkets and fruit shops, as ripe bananas are often sold very cheaply. This cake tastes really delicious the day after it has been made – the sponge solidifies slightly yet does not lose any moisture. Eat within 3–4 days.

Coffee & Pecan Cake

1　Preheat the oven to 190°C/375°F/Gas Mark 5, 10 minutes before baking. Lightly oil and line the bases of two 18 cm/7 inch sandwich tins with greaseproof or baking paper. Sift the flour and reserve.

2　Beat the butter or margarine and sugar together until light and creamy. Dissolve the coffee in 2 tablespoons of hot water and allow to cool.

3　Lightly mix the eggs with the coffee liquid. Gradually beat into the creamed butter and sugar, adding a little of the sifted flour with each addition. Fold in the pecans, then divide the mixture between the prepared tins and bake in the preheated oven for 20–25 minutes, or until well risen and firm to the touch.

4　Leave to cool in the tins for 5 minutes before turning out and cooling on a wire rack.

5　To make the icing, blend together the coffee and cocoa powder with enough boiling water to make a stiff paste. Beat into the butter and icing sugar.

6　Sandwich the two cakes together using half the icing. Spread the remaining icing over the top of the cake and decorate with the whole pecans to serve. Store in an airtight tin.

Ingredients

CUTS INTO 8 SLICES

175 g/6 oz self-raising flour
125 g/4 oz butter or margarine
175 g/6 oz golden caster sugar
1 tbsp instant coffee powder
　or granules
2 large eggs
50 g/2 oz pecans, roughly chopped

For the icing:

1 tsp instant coffee powder
　or granules
1 tsp cocoa powder
75 g/3 oz unsalted butter, softened
175 g/6 oz icing sugar, sifted
whole pecans, to decorate

Helpful hint

To bake in bulk, follow the recipe up to step 4, then when the cakes have cooled wrap in greaseproof paper or foil and freeze. Defrost slowly at room temperature when needed.

Gingerbread

1 Preheat the oven to 150°C/300°F/Gas Mark 2, 10 minutes before baking. Lightly oil and line the base of a 20.5 cm/8 inch deep round cake tin with greaseproof or baking paper.

2 In a saucepan, gently heat the butter or margarine, black treacle and sugar, stirring occasionally until the butter melts. Leave to cool slightly.

3 Sift the flour and ground ginger into a large bowl. Make a well in the centre, then pour in the treacle mixture. Reserve 1 tablespoon of the milk, then pour the rest into the treacle mixture. Stir together lightly until mixed.

4 Beat the eggs together, then stir into the mixture.

5 Dissolve the bicarbonate of soda in the remaining 1 tablespoon of warmed milk and add to the mixture. Beat the mixture until well mixed and free of lumps.

6 Pour into the prepared tin and bake in the preheated oven for 1 hour, or until well risen and a skewer inserted into the centre comes out clean.

7 Cool in the tin, then remove. Slice the stem ginger into thin slivers and sprinkle over the cake. Drizzle with the syrup and serve.

Ingredients CUTS INTO 8 SLICES

175 g/6 oz butter or margarine
225 g/8 oz black treacle
50 g/2 oz dark muscovado sugar
350 g/12 oz plain flour
2 tsp ground ginger
150 ml/$^1/_4$ pint milk, warmed
2 medium eggs
1 tsp bicarbonate of soda
1 piece of stem ginger in syrup
1 tbsp stem ginger syrup

Food fact

There are many different types of gingerbread, ranging in colour from a deep rich dark brown to a light golden. This is due to the type of treacle and the amount of bicarbonate of soda used. One well-known gingerbread from Yorkshire is Parkin which uses both golden syrup and black treacle.

Carrot Cake

1   Preheat the oven to 150°C/300°F/Gas Mark 2, 10 minutes before baking. Lightly oil and line the base of a 15 cm/6 inch deep square cake tin with greaseproof or baking paper.

2   Sift the flour, spices, baking powder and bicarbonate of soda together into a large bowl.

3   Stir in the dark muscovado sugar and mix together.

4   Lightly whisk the oil and eggs together, then gradually stir into the flour and sugar mixture. Stir well.

5   Add the carrots and walnuts. Mix thoroughly, then pour into the prepared cake tin. Bake in the preheated oven for $1^1/_4$ hours, or until light and springy to the touch and a skewer inserted into the centre of the cake comes out clean.

6   Remove from the oven and allow to cool in the tin for 5 minutes before turning out on to a wire rack. Reserve until cold.

7   To make the icing, beat together the cream cheese, orange rind, orange juice and vanilla essence. Sift the icing sugar and stir into the cream cheese mixture.

8   When cold, discard the lining paper, spread the cream cheese icing over the top and serve cut into squares.

Ingredients   CUTS INTO 8 SLICES

200 g/7 oz plain flour
$^1/_2$ tsp ground cinnamon
$^1/_2$ tsp freshly grated nutmeg
1 tsp baking powder
1 tsp bicarbonate of soda
150 g/5 oz dark muscovado sugar
200 ml/7 fl oz vegetable oil
3 medium eggs
225 g/8 oz carrots, peeled and
     roughly grated
50 g/2 oz chopped walnuts

For the icing:
175 g/6 oz cream cheese
finely grated rind of 1 orange
1 tbsp orange juice
1 tsp vanilla essence
125 g/4 oz icing sugar

Tasty tip
For a fruitier cake, add 1 grated apple and 50 g/2 oz of dried sultanas in step 5. To plump up the sultanas, soak for an hour in 300 ml/$^1/_2$ pint of cold tea.

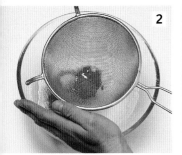

Jammy Buns

1 Preheat the oven to 190°C/375°F/Gas Mark 5, 10 minutes before baking. Lightly oil a large baking sheet.

2 Sift the flours and baking powder together into a large bowl, then tip in the grains remaining in the sieve.

3 Cut the butter or margarine into small pieces. It is easier to do this when the butter is in the flour as it helps stop the butter from sticking to the knife.

4 Rub the butter into the flours until it resembles coarse breadcrumbs. Stir in the sugar and cranberries.

5 Using a round bladed knife, stir in the beaten egg and milk. Mix to form a firm dough. Divide the mixture into 12 and roll into balls.

6 Place the dough balls on the baking tray, leaving enough space for expansion. Press the thumb into the centre of each ball making a small hollow.

7 Spoon a little of the jam into each hollow. Pinch lightly to seal the tops.

8 Bake in the preheated oven for 20–25 minutes, or until golden brown. Cool on a wire rack and serve.

Ingredients   MAKES 12

175 g/6 oz plain flour
175 g/6 oz wholemeal flour
2 tsp baking powder
150 g/5 oz butter or margarine
125 g/4 oz golden caster sugar
50 g/2 oz dried cranberries
1 large egg, beaten
1 tbsp milk
4–5 tbsp seedless raspberry jam

Tasty tip

In this recipe, any type of jam can be used. However, look for one with a high fruit content. Alternatively replace the jam with a fruit compote. Simply boil some fruit with a little sugar and water, then leave to cool before placing inside the buns.

4

6

7

Whisked Sponge Cake

1　Preheat the oven to 200°C/400°F/Gas Mark 6, 15 minutes before baking. Mix 1 teaspoon of the flour and 1 teaspoon of the sugar together. Lightly oil two 18 cm/7 inch sandwich tins and dust lightly with the sugar and flour.

2　Place the eggs in a large heatproof bowl. Add the sugar, then place over a saucepan of gently simmering water ensuring that the base of the bowl does not touch the hot water. Using an electric whisk, beat the sugar and eggs until they become light and fluffy. The whisk should leave a trail in the mixture when it is lifted out.

3　Remove the bowl from the saucepan of water, add the vanilla essence and continue beating for 2–3 minutes. Sift the flour gently into the egg mixture and, using a metal spoon or rubber spatula, carefully fold in, taking care not to overmix and remove all the air that has been whisked in.

4　Divide the mixture between the two prepared cake tins. Tap lightly on the work surface to remove any air bubbles. Bake in the preheated oven for 20–25 minutes, or until golden. Test that the cake is ready by gently pressing the centre with a clean finger – it should spring back. Leave to cool in the tins for 5 minutes, then turn out on to a wire rack. Blend the jam and the crushed raspberries together. When the cakes are cold spread over the jam mixture and sandwich together. Dust the top with icing sugar and serve.

Ingredients

CUTS INTO 6 SLICES

125 g/4 oz plain flour, plus 1 tsp
175 g/6 oz caster sugar, plus 1 tsp
3 medium eggs
1 tsp vanilla essence
4 tbsp raspberry jam
50 g/2 oz fresh raspberries, crushed
icing sugar, to dust

Tasty tip

For a creamier low-fat filling, mix the crushed raspberries or strawberries with 4 tablespoons each of low-fat Greek yogurt and low-fat crème fraîche.

Marble Cake

1. Preheat the oven to 190°C/375°F/Gas Mark 5, 10 minutes before baking. Lightly oil and line the base of a 20.5 cm/8 inch deep round cake tin with greaseproof or baking paper. In a large bowl, cream the butter or margarine and sugar together until light and fluffy. Beat the eggs together. Beat into the creamed mixture a little at a time, beating well between each addition. When all the egg has been added, fold in the flour with a metal spoon or rubber spatula. Divide the mixture equally between two bowls. Beat the grated orange rind into one of the bowls with a little of the orange juice. Mix the cocoa powder with the remaining orange juice until smooth, then add to the other bowl and beat well.

2. Spoon the mixture into the tin, in alternate spoonfuls. When all the cake mixture is in the tin, take a skewer and swirl it in the two mixtures. Tap the base of the tin on the work surface to level the mixture. Bake for 50 minutes, or until cooked and a skewer inserted into the centre of the cake comes out clean. Remove from the oven and leave in the tin for a few minutes before cooling on a wire rack. Discard the lining paper.

3. For the topping, place the orange zest and juice with the granulated sugar in a small saucepan and heat gently until the sugar has dissolved. Bring to the boil and simmer gently for 3–4 minutes, until the juice is syrupy. Pour over the cooled cake and serve when cool. Otherwise, store in an airtight tin.

Ingredients
CUTS INTO 8 SLICES

225 g/8 oz butter or margarine
225 g/8 oz caster sugar
4 medium eggs
225 g/8 oz self-raising flour, sifted
juice and finely grated rind
   of 1 orange
25 g/1 oz cocoa powder, sifted

For the topping:
zest and juice of 1 orange
1 tbsp granulated sugar

Helpful hint
This cake has a wonderful combination of rich chocolate and orangey sponge. It is important not to swirl too much in step 2, as the desired effect is to have blocks of different coloured sponge.

Biscuits, Cookies, Brownies & Traybakes

This section includes recipes for everyone's favourite treats that are so easy anyone can make them. Whether you fancy the classic Chocolate Chip Cookies and Oatmeal Raisin Cookies, or the more indulgent Chocolate Fudge Brownies or Pecan Caramel Millionaire's Shortbread, this section will show you how to bake them.

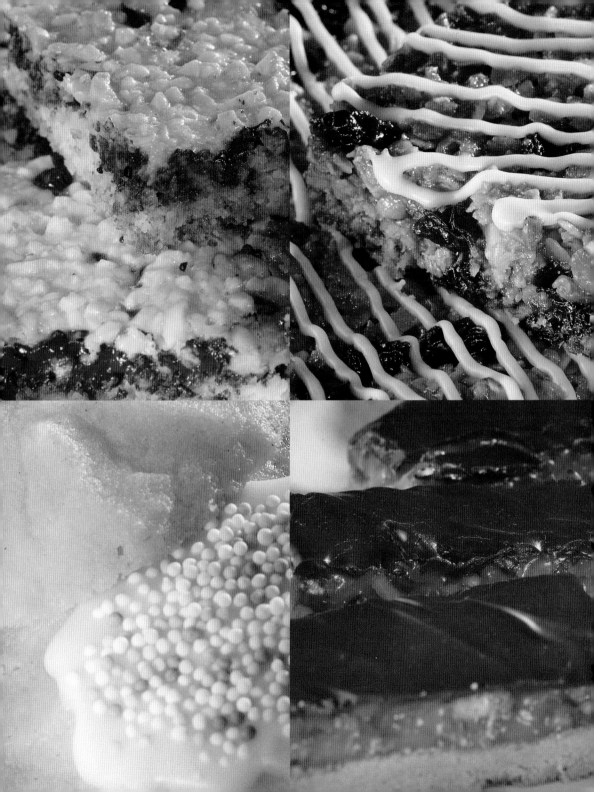

Chocolate Chip Cookies

1 Preheat the oven to 190°C/375°F/Gas Mark 5, 10 minutes before baking. Lightly oil a large baking sheet.

2 In a large bowl, sift together the flour, salt, baking powder and bicarbonate of soda.

3 Cut the butter or margarine into small pieces and add to the flour mixture. Using two knives or your fingertips, rub in the butter or margarine until the mixture resembles coarse breadcrumbs.

4 Add the light brown sugar, golden syrup and chocolate chips. Mix together until a smooth dough forms.

5 Shape the mixture into small balls and arrange on the baking sheet, leaving enough space to allow them to expand. (These cookies do not increase in size by a great deal, but allow a little space for expansion.)

6 Flatten the mixture slightly with the fingertips or the heel of the hand. Bake in the preheated oven for 12–15 minutes, or until golden and cooked through.

7 Allow to cool slightly, then transfer the biscuits on to a wire rack to cool. Serve when cold or otherwise store in an airtight tin.

Ingredients   MAKES 36

175 g/6 oz plain flour
pinch of salt
1 tsp baking powder
$^1/_4$ tsp bicarbonate of soda
75 g/3 oz butter or margarine
50 g/2 oz soft light brown sugar
3 tbsp golden syrup
125 g/4 oz chocolate chips

Tasty tip

This is a good basic cookie recipe to which many ingredients, like nuts, glacé cherries, chopped angelica, banana chips, dried cranberries or raisins can be added instead of chocolate chips.

3

6

7

Chocolate Florentines

1 Preheat the oven to 180°C/350°F/Gas Mark 4, 10 minutes before baking. Lightly oil a baking sheet.

2 Melt the butter or margarine with the sugar and double cream in a small saucepan over a very low heat. Do not boil.

3 Remove from the heat and stir in the almonds, hazelnuts, sultanas and cherries.

4 Drop teaspoonfuls of the mixture on to the baking sheet. Transfer to the preheated oven and bake for 10 minutes, until golden.

5 Leave the biscuits to cool on the baking sheet for about 5 minutes, then carefully transfer to a wire rack to cool.

6 Melt the plain, milk and white chocolates in separate bowls, either in the microwave following the manufacturer's instructions or in a small bowl, placed over a saucepan of gently simmering water.

7 Spread one third of the biscuits with the plain chocolate, one third with the milk chocolate and one third with the white chocolate.

8 Mark out wavy lines on the chocolate when almost set with the tines of a fork. Or dip some of the biscuits in chocolate to half-coat, and serve.

Ingredients   MAKES 20

125 g/4 oz butter or margarine
125 g/4 oz soft light brown sugar
1 tbsp double cream
50 g/2 oz blanched almonds,
    roughly chopped
50 g/2 oz hazelnuts,
    roughly chopped
75 g/3 oz sultanas
50 g/2 oz glacé cherries,
    roughly chopped
50 g/2 oz plain, dark chocolate,
    roughly chopped or broken
50 g/2 oz milk chocolate,
    roughly chopped or broken
50 g/2 oz white chocolate,
    roughly chopped or broken

Tasty tip

Rich and fruity, these Florentines rely on their raw ingredients, so try to use a good-quality chocolate and natural glacé cherries, which have a fruitier taste and are more natural in colour.

Ginger Snaps

1   Preheat the oven to 190°C/375°F/Gas Mark 5, 10 minutes before baking. Lightly oil a baking sheet.

2   Cream together the butter or margarine and the sugar until light and fluffy.

3   Warm the treacle in the microwave for 30–40 seconds, then add gradually to the butter mixture with the egg. Beat until well combined.

4   In a separate bowl, sift the flour, bicarbonate of soda, salt, ground ginger, ground cloves and ground cinnamon. Add to the butter mixture and mix together to form a firm dough.

5   Chill in the refrigerator for 1 hour. Shape the dough into small balls and roll in the granulated sugar. Place well apart on the oiled baking sheet.

6   Sprinkle the baking sheet with a little water and transfer to the preheated oven.

7   Bake for 12 minutes, until golden and crisp. Transfer to a wire rack to cool and serve.

Ingredients   MAKES 40

300 g/11 oz butter or margarine, softened
225 g/8 oz soft light brown sugar
75 g/3 oz black treacle
1 medium egg
400 g/14 oz plain flour
2 tsp bicarbonate of soda
$\frac{1}{2}$ tsp salt
1 tsp ground ginger
1 tsp ground cloves
1 tsp ground cinnamon
50 g/2 oz granulated sugar

Tasty tip

Ginger snaps are great biscuits to use in other recipes. Try crushing them, mixing with melted butter and using as the base for a cheesecake.

Oatmeal Raisin Cookies

1 Preheat the oven to 200°C/400°F/Gas Mark 6, 15 minutes before baking. Lightly oil a baking sheet.

2 Mix together the flour, oats, ground ginger, baking powder, bicarbonate of soda, sugar and the raisins in a large bowl.

3 In another bowl, mix the egg, oil and milk together. Make a well in the centre of the dry ingredients and pour in the egg mixture.

4 Mix together well with either a fork or a wooden spoon to make a soft, but not sticky, dough.

5 Place spoonfuls of the dough well apart on the oiled baking sheet and flatten the tops down slightly with the tines of a fork.

6 Transfer the biscuits to the preheated oven and bake for 10–12 minutes until golden.

7 Remove from the oven, leave to cool for 2–3 minutes, then transfer the biscuits to a wire rack to cool. Serve when cold or otherwise store in an airtight tin.

Ingredients   MAKES 24

175 g/6 oz plain flour
150 g/5 oz rolled oats
1 tsp ground ginger
$^1/_2$ tsp baking powder
$^1/_2$ tsp bicarbonate of soda
125 g/4 oz soft light brown sugar
50 g/2 oz raisins
1 medium egg, lightly beaten
150 ml/$^1/_4$ pint vegetable or
    sunflower oil
4 tbsp milk

Tasty tip

If desired, add 50 g/2 oz of roughly chopped mixed nuts and replace half the raisins with dried cranberries or cherries.

Food fact

This dough can be made, wrapped in clingfilm then stored in the refrigerator for up to 1 week before baking. When ready to bake, simply cut off the dough and bake as above.

Almond Macaroons

1 Preheat the oven to 150°C/300°F/Gas Mark 2, 10 minutes before baking. Line a baking sheet with the rice paper.

2 Mix the caster sugar, ground almonds, ground rice and almond essence together and reserve.

3 Whisk the egg white until stiff then gently fold in the caster sugar mixture with a metal spoon or rubber spatula.

4 Mix to form a stiff, but not sticky, paste. If the mixture is very sticky, add a little extra ground almonds.

5 Place small spoonfuls of the mixture, about the size of an apricot, well apart on the rice paper.

6 Place a half-blanched almond in the centre of each. Place in the preheated oven and bake for 25 minutes, or until just pale golden.

7 Remove the biscuits from the oven and leave to cool for a few minutes on the baking sheet. Cut or tear the rice paper around the macaroons to release them. Once cold, serve or store them in an airtight tin.

Ingredients   MAKES 12

rice paper
125 g/4 oz caster sugar
50 g/2 oz ground almonds
1 tsp ground rice
2–3 drops almond essence
1 medium egg white
8 blanched almonds, halved

Tasty tip

Rice paper is an edible paper made from the pith of the Chinese tree. These macaroons are deliciously chewy and are fantastic when broken up and sprinkled in desserts such as trifles. Serve with cream and tart, fresh fruits such as raspberries.

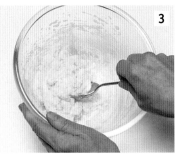
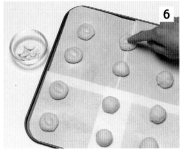

Pumpkin Cookies with Brown Butter Glaze

1 Preheat the oven to 190°C/375°F/Gas Mark 5, 10 minutes before baking. Lightly oil a baking sheet and reserve.

2 Using an electric mixer, beat the butter until light and fluffy. Add the flour, sugar, pumpkin and beaten egg and beat with the mixer until well combined.

3 Stir in the ground cinnamon and 1 teaspoon of the vanilla essence, then sift in the baking powder, bicarbonate of soda and grated nutmeg. Beat the mixture until well combined, scraping down the sides of the bowl.

4 Add the wholemeal flour, chopped nuts and raisins to the mixture and fold in with a metal spoon or rubber spatula until mixed thoroughly together.

5 Place teaspoonfuls about 5 cm/2 inches apart on to the baking sheet. Bake in the preheated oven for 10–12 minutes, or until the cookie edges are firm.

6 Remove the biscuits from the oven and leave to cool on a wire rack. Meanwhile, melt the butter in a small saucepan over a medium heat, until pale and just turning golden brown.

7 Remove from the heat. Add the sugar, remaining vanilla essence and milk, stirring. Drizzle over the cooled cookies and serve.

Ingredients   MAKES 48

125 g/4 oz butter, softened
150 g/5 oz plain flour
175 g/6 oz soft light brown sugar, lightly packed
225 g/8 oz canned pumpkin or cooked pumpkin
1 medium egg, beaten
2 tsp ground cinnamon
$2^{1}/_{2}$ tsp vanilla essence
$^{1}/_{2}$ tsp baking powder
$^{1}/_{2}$ tsp bicarbonate of soda
$^{1}/_{2}$ tsp freshly grated nutmeg
125 g/4 oz wholemeal flour
75 g/3 oz pecans, roughly chopped
100 g/$3^{1}/_{2}$ oz raisins
50 g/2 oz unsalted butter
225 g/8 oz icing sugar
2 tbsp milk

Spiced Palmier Biscuits with Apple Purée

1 Preheat the oven to 200˚C/400˚F/Gas Mark 6, 15 minutes before baking. Roll out the pastry on a lightly floured surface to form a 25.5 x 30.5 cm/10 x 12 inch rectangle. Trim the edges with a small, sharp knife.

2 Sift together the caster sugar, icing sugar, cinnamon, ginger and nutmeg into a bowl. Generously dust both sides of the pastry with a quarter of the sugar mixture. With a long edge facing you, fold either side halfway towards the centre. Dust with a third of the remaining sugar mixture. Fold each side again so that they almost meet in the centre and dust again with half the remaining sugar mixture. Fold the two sides together down the centre to give six layers altogether. Wrap the pastry in clingfilm and refrigerate for 1–2 hours until firm. Reserve the remaining spiced sugar.

3 Remove the pastry from the refrigerator, unwrap and roll in the remaining sugar to give a good coating. Cut the roll into about 20 thin slices and place on to a baking sheet. Bake for 10 minutes, turn the biscuits and cook for a further 5–10 minutes, or until golden and crisp. Remove from the oven and transfer to a wire rack. Allow to cool completely.

4 Meanwhile, combine the remaining ingredients in a saucepan. Cover and cook gently for 15 minutes until the apple is completely soft. Stir well and allow to cool. Serve the palmiers with a spoonful of the apple purée and the whipped cream.

Ingredients   MAKES 20

250 g/9 oz prepared puff pastry,
   thawed if frozen
40 g/1¹/₂ oz caster sugar
25 g/1 oz icing sugar
1 tsp ground cinnamon
¹/₄ tsp ground ginger
¹/₄ tsp freshly grated nutmeg
450 g/1 lb Bramley cooking apples,
   roughly chopped
50 g/2 oz sugar
25 g/1 oz raisins
25 g/1 oz dried cherries
zest of 1 orange
double cream, lightly whipped,
   to serve

Food fact

Palmiers are so called as they are thought to resemble palm leaves – *palmier* being the French word for a palm tree. Palmiers are often served sandwiched together with whipped cream and jam.

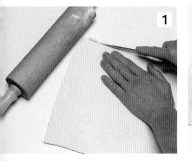

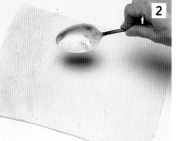

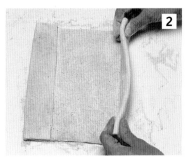

Peanut Butter Truffle Cookies

1 Preheat the oven to 180°C/350°F/Gas Mark 4, 10 minutes before baking. Make the chocolate filling by breaking the chocolate into small pieces and placing in a heatproof bowl.

2 Put the double cream into a saucepan and heat to boiling point. Immediately pour this over the chocolate. Leave to stand for 1–2 minutes, then stir until smooth. Set aside to cool until firm enough to scoop. Do not refrigerate.

3 Lightly oil a baking sheet. Cream together the butter or margarine and the sugar until light and fluffy. Blend in the peanut butter, followed by the golden syrup and milk.

4 Sift together the flour and bicarbonate of soda. Add to the peanut butter mixture, mix well and knead until smooth.

5 Flatten 1–2 tablespoons of cookie mixture on a chopping board.

6 Put a spoonful of the chocolate mixture into the centre of the cookie dough, then fold the dough around the chocolate to enclose completely. Put the balls on to the baking sheet and flatten slightly. Bake in the preheated oven for 10–12 minutes until golden.

7 Remove from the oven and transfer to a wire rack to cool completely and serve.

Ingredients   MAKES 18

125 g/4 oz plain dark chocolate
150 ml/¼ pint double cream
125 g/4 oz butter or margarine, softened
125 g/4 oz caster sugar
125 g/4 oz crunchy or smooth peanut butter
4 tbsp golden syrup
1 tbsp milk
225 g/8 oz plain flour
½ tsp bicarbonate of soda

Helpful hint

Measure golden syrup either by warming a metal measuring spoon in boiling water, then dipping it into the syrup, or placing the tin in a warm oven or saucepan half-filled with hot water.

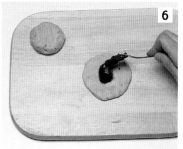

Whipped Shortbread

1 Preheat the oven to 180°C/350°F/Gas Mark 4, 10 minutes before baking. Lightly oil a baking sheet.

2 Cream the butter and icing sugar until fluffy. Gradually add the flour and continue beating for a further 2–3 minutes until it is smooth and light.

3 Roll into balls and place on a baking sheet. Cover half the dough mixture with hundreds and thousands, sugar strands, chocolate drops or silver balls. Keep the other half plain.

4 Bake in the preheated oven for 6–8 minutes, until the bottoms are lightly browned. Remove from the oven and transfer to a wire rack to cool.

5 Sift the icing sugar into a small bowl. Add the lemon juice and blend until a smooth icing forms.

6 Using a small spoon swirl the icing over the cooled plain cookies. Decorate with either the extra hundreds and thousands, chocolate drops or silver balls and serve.

Ingredients   MAKES 36

225 g/8 oz butter, softened
75 g/3 oz icing sugar
175 g/6 oz plain flour
hundreds and thousands
sugar strands
chocolate drops
silver balls
50 g/2 oz icing sugar
2–3 tsp lemon juice

Helpful hint

Although these biscuits have the flavour of classic shortbread, the texture is much lighter. They literally melt in the mouth. These biscuits are great for children. However, for a smarter-looking biscuit which is more appealing to adults, spoon the mixture into a piping bag fitted with a large star nozzle and pipe the biscuits on to the baking sheet. Bake as above.

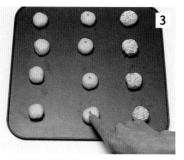

Oatmeal Coconut Cookies

1 Preheat the oven to 180°C/350°F/Gas Mark 4, 10 minutes before baking. Lightly oil a baking sheet.

2 Cream together the butter or margarine and sugars until light and fluffy.

3 Gradually stir in the egg and vanilla essence and beat until well blended.

4 Sift together the flour, baking powder and bicarbonate of soda in another bowl.

5 Add to the butter and sugar mixture and beat together until smooth. Fold in the rolled oats and coconut with a metal spoon or rubber spatula.

6 Roll heaped teaspoonfuls of the mixture into balls and place on the baking sheet about 5 cm/2 inches apart and flatten each ball slightly with the heel of the hand.

7 Transfer to the preheated oven and bake for 12–15 minutes, until just golden.

8 Remove from the oven and transfer the biscuits to a wire rack to completely cool and serve.

Ingredients   MAKES 40

225 g/8 oz butter or margarine
125 g/4 oz soft light brown sugar
125 g/4 oz caster sugar
1 large egg, lightly beaten
1 tsp vanilla essence
225 g/8 oz plain flour
1 tsp baking powder
$^1/_2$ tsp bicarbonate of soda
125 g/4 oz rolled oats
75 g/3 oz desiccated coconut

Helpful hint

The raising agent in this recipe, bicarbonate of soda, lightens the texture of these biscuits, resulting in a crisp yet melting result. These biscuits will last for 3–4 days if stored in an airtight tin or jar.

3

5

6

Chocolate Biscuit Bars

1 Lightly oil a 20.5 cm/8 inch square tin and line with clingfilm.

2 Place the sultanas into a small bowl and pour over the brandy, if using. Leave to soak for 20–30 minutes.

3 Meanwhile, break the chocolate into small pieces and put into a heatproof bowl. Place the bowl over a saucepan of simmering water, making sure that the bottom of the bowl does not touch the water. Leave the chocolate until melted, stirring occasionally. Remove from the heat.

4 Add the butter, golden syrup and double cream to a small saucepan and heat until the butter has melted.

5 Remove the saucepan from the heat and add the melted chocolate, biscuits, nuts, cherries, orange zest, sultanas and the brandy mixture.

6 Mix thoroughly and pour into the prepared tin. Smooth the top and chill in the refrigerator for at least 4 hours, or until firm.

7 Turn out the cake and remove the clingfilm. Dust liberally with the cocoa powder then cut into bars to serve. Store lightly covered in the refrigerator.

Ingredients MAKES 20 SLICES

50 g/2 oz sultanas
3–4 tbsp brandy (optional)
100 g/3$^1/_2$ oz plain dark chocolate
125 g/4 oz unsalted butter
2 tbsp golden syrup
90 ml/3 fl oz double cream
6 digestive biscuits, roughly crushed
50 g/2 oz shelled pistachio nuts,
    toasted and roughly chopped
50 g/2 oz blanched almonds, toasted
    and roughly chopped
50 g/2 oz glacé cherries,
    roughly chopped
grated zest of 1 orange
cocoa powder, sifted

Helpful hint

You may find these bars slice more easily if you heat the knife first. Run the blade of the knife under hot water and wipe dry with a clean tea towel, then slice.

Miracle Bars

1 Preheat the oven to 180°C/350°F/Gas Mark 4, 10 minutes before baking. Generously butter a 23 cm/9 inch square tin and line with non-stick baking paper.

2 Pour the butter into the prepared tin and sprinkle the biscuit crumbs over in an even layer.

3 Add the chocolate chips, coconut and nuts in even layers and drizzle over the condensed milk.

4 Transfer the tin to the preheated oven and bake for 30 minutes, until golden brown. Allow to cool in the tin, then cut into 12 squares and serve.

Ingredients   MAKES 12

100 g/3½ oz butter, melted,
    plus 1–2 tsp extra for oiling
125 g/4 oz digestive biscuit crumbs
175 g/6 oz chocolate chips
75 g/3 oz shredded or
    desiccated coconut
125 g/4 oz chopped mixed nuts
400 g can sweetened condensed milk

Food fact

Condensed milk is pasteurised, homogenised milk that has been reduced to about two thirds of its original volume by boiling under strictly controlled conditions. It is no longer advised to boil the can of condensed milk when wishing to convert the milk to a golden toffee filling as in banoffee pie. Instead, either place the milk in a heavy-based saucepan and boil gently, or place in a glass bowl, cover with clingfilm, pierce and cook on medium for 1–2 minutes at a time in a microwave. Keep checking to ensure the milk does not burn.

Apple & Cinnamon Crumble Bars

1 Preheat the oven to 190°C/375°F/Gas Mark 5, 10 minutes before baking. Place the apples, raisins, sugar, cinnamon and lemon zest into a saucepan over a low heat.

2 Cover and cook for about 15 minutes, stirring occasionally, until the apple is cooked through. Remove the cover and stir well to break up the apple completely with a wooden spoon.

3 Cook for a further 15–30 minutes over a very low heat until reduced, thickened and slightly darkened. Allow to cool. Lightly oil and line a 20.5 cm/8 inch square cake tin with greaseproof or baking paper.

4 Mix together the flour, sugar, bicarbonate of soda, rolled oats and butter until well combined and crumbly.

5 Spread half the flour mixture into the bottom of the prepared tin and press down. Pour over the apple mixture.

6 Sprinkle over the remaining flour mixture and press down lightly. Bake in the preheated oven for 30–35 minutes, until golden brown.

7 Remove from the oven and allow to cool before cutting into slices. Serve the bars warm or cold with crème fraîche or whipped cream.

Ingredients   MAKES 16

450 g/1 lb Bramley cooking apples, roughly chopped
50 g/2 oz raisins
50 g/2 oz caster sugar
1 tsp ground cinnamon
zest of 1 lemon
200 g/7 oz plain flour
250 g/9 oz soft light brown sugar
$^1/_2$ tsp bicarbonate of soda
150 g/5 oz rolled oats
150 g/5 oz butter, melted
crème fraîche or whipped cream, to serve

Tasty tip

The apple filling in this recipe is very similar to American apple butter. To make apple butter, cook the filling in step 2 for a further 30 minutes over a very low heat, stirring often. When reduced to one third of its original volume (it should be quite dark) then it is ready. It is also delicious spread on toast.

Lemon Bars

1 Preheat the oven to 170°C/325°F/Gas Mark 3, 10 minutes before baking. Lightly oil and line a 20.5 cm/8 inch square cake tin with greaseproof or baking paper.

2 Rub together the flour and butter until the mixture resembles breadcrumbs. Stir in the granulated sugar and mix.

3 Turn the mixture into the prepared tin and press down firmly. Bake in the preheated oven for 20 minutes, until pale golden.

4 Meanwhile, in a food processor, mix together the caster sugar, flour, baking powder, salt, eggs, lemon juice and rind until smooth. Pour over the prepared base.

5 Transfer to the preheated oven and bake for a further 20–25 minutes, until nearly set but still a bit wobbly in the centre. Remove from the oven and cool in the tin on a wire rack.

6 Dust with icing sugar and cut into squares. Serve cold or store in an airtight tin.

Ingredients MAKES 24

175 g/6 oz flour
125 g/4 oz butter
50 g/2 oz granulated sugar
200 g/7 oz caster sugar
2 tbsp flour
$^1/_2$ tsp baking powder
$^1/_4$ tsp salt
2 medium eggs, lightly beaten
juice and finely grated rind of
   1 lemon
sifted icing sugar, to decorate

Food fact

Baking powder is a chemically prepared raising agent consisting of cream of tartar and bicarbonate of soda, which is then mixed with a dried starch or flour. It is very important to measure accurately, otherwise the mixture could either not rise, or rise too quickly and then collapse, and give a sour taste to the dish.

2

4

6

Lemon-iced Ginger Squares

1   Preheat the oven to 200°C/400°F/Gas Mark 6, 15 minutes before baking. Lightly oil a 20.5 cm/8 inch square cake tin and sprinkle with a little flour.

2   Mix together the caster sugar, butter and treacle. Stir in the egg whites.

3   Mix together the flour, bicarbonate of soda, cloves, cinnamon, ginger and salt.

4   Stir the flour mixture and buttermilk alternately into the butter mixture until well blended.

5   Spoon into the prepared tin and bake in the preheated oven for 35 minutes, or until a skewer inserted into the centre of the cake comes out clean.

6   Remove from the oven and allow to cool for 5 minutes in the tin before turning out on to a wire rack over a large plate. Using a cocktail stick make holes in the top of the cake.

7   Meanwhile, mix together the icing sugar with enough lemon juice to make a smooth, pourable icing.

8   Carefully pour the icing over the hot cake, then leave until cold. Cut the ginger cake into squares and serve.

Ingredients   MAKES 12

225 g/8 oz caster sugar
50 g/2 oz butter, melted
2 tbsp black treacle
2 medium egg whites, lightly whisked
225 g/8 oz plain flour
1 tsp bicarbonate of soda
$1/2$ tsp ground cloves
1 tsp ground cinnamon
$1/4$ tsp ground ginger
pinch of salt
225 ml/8 fl oz buttermilk
175 g/6 oz icing sugar
lemon juice

Food fact

Buttermilk is the liquid that remains after churning cream into butter. It is considered a healthy alternative to sour cream as it does not contain the fat of the cream. It contains lactic acid and when mixed with bicarbonate of soda it acts as a raising agent.

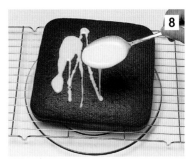

Pecan Caramel Millionaire's Shortbread

1 Preheat the oven to 180°C/350°F/Gas Mark 4, 10 minutes before baking. Lightly oil and line an 18 x 28 cm/7 x 11 inch cake tin with greaseproof or baking paper.

2 Cream together the butter, peanut butter and sugar until light. Sift in the cornflour and flour together and mix in to make a smooth dough. Press the mixture into the prepared tin and prick all over with a fork. Bake in the preheated oven for 20 minutes, until just golden. Remove from the oven.

3 Meanwhile, for the topping, combine the sugar, butter, golden syrup, glucose, water and milk in a heavy-based saucepan. Stir constantly over a low heat without boiling until the sugar has dissolved. Increase the heat, boil steadily, stirring constantly, for about 10 minutes until the mixture turns a golden caramel colour. Remove from the heat and add the pecans. Pour over the shortbread base. Allow to cool, then refrigerate for at least 1 hour.

4 Break the chocolate into small pieces and put into a heatproof bowl with the butter. Place over a saucepan of barely simmering water, ensuring that the bowl does not come into contact with the water. Leave until melted, then stir together well.

5 Remove the shortbread from the refrigerator and pour the chocolate evenly over the top, spreading thinly to cover. Leave to set, cut into squares and serve.

Ingredients   SERVES 20

125 g/4 oz butter, softened
2 tbsp smooth peanut butter
75 g/3 oz caster sugar
75 g/3 oz cornflour
175 g/6 oz plain flour

For the topping:

200 g/7 oz caster sugar
125 g/4 oz butter
2 tbsp golden syrup
75 g/3 oz liquid glucose
75 ml/3 fl oz water
400 g can sweetened
   condensed milk
175 g/6 oz pecans, roughly chopped
75 g/3 oz plain dark chocolate
1 tbsp butter

Tasty tip

Any type of nut can be used in this recipe. Why not try replacing the pecans with a variety of chopped walnuts, almonds and brazil nuts?

Fruit & Nut Flapjacks

1   Preheat the oven to 180°C/350°F/Gas Mark 4, 10 minutes before baking. Lightly oil a 23 cm/9 inch square cake tin.

2   Melt the butter or margarine with the sugar and syrup in a small saucepan over a low heat. Remove from the heat.

3   Add the raisins, walnuts and oats to the syrup mixture and stir well.

4   Spoon evenly into the prepared tin and press down well. Transfer to the preheated oven and bake for 20–25 minutes.

5   Remove from the oven and leave to cool in the tin. Cut into bars while still warm.

6   Sift the icing sugar into a small bowl then gradually beat in the lemon juice a little at a time to form a thin icing.

7   Place into an icing bag fitted with a writing nozzle then pipe thin lines over the flapjacks. Allow to cool and serve.

Ingredients   SERVES 12

75 g/3 oz butter or margarine
125 g/4 oz soft light brown sugar
3 tbsp golden syrup
50 g/2 oz raisins
50 g/2 oz walnuts, roughly chopped
175 g/6 oz rolled oats
50 g/2 oz icing sugar
1–1¹/₂ tbsp lemon juice

Tasty tip

These flapjacks are packed with energy, but why not increase the nutritional value by adding a few tablespoons of seeds, such as sesame, sunflower and pumpkin seeds, then add some chopped up ready-to-eat fruit such as apricot, pineapple or mango? You can also add chocolate chips and chopped glacé fruits as well as currants and sultanas.

Chocolate Fudge Brownies

1   Preheat the oven to 180°C/350°F/Gas Mark 4, 10 minutes before baking. Lightly oil and line a 20.5 cm/8 inch square cake tin with greaseproof or baking paper.

2   Slowly melt the butter and chocolate together in a heatproof bowl set over a saucepan of simmering water. Transfer the mixture to a large bowl.

3   Stir in the sugar and vanilla essence, then stir in the eggs. Sift over the flour and fold together well with a metal spoon or rubber spatula. Pour into the prepared tin.

4   Transfer to the preheated oven and bake for 30 minutes until just set. Remove the cooked mixture from the oven and leave to cool in the tin before turning it out on to a wire rack.

5   Sift the icing sugar and cocoa powder into a small bowl and make a well in the centre.

6   Place the butter in the well then gradually add about 2 tablespoons of hot water. Mix to form a smooth, spreadable icing.

7   Pour the icing over the cooked mixture. Allow the icing to set before cutting into squares. Serve the brownies when they are cold.

Ingredients   MAKES 16

125 g/4 oz butter
175 g/6 oz plain dark chocolate, roughly chopped or broken
225 g/8 oz caster sugar
2 tsp vanilla essence
2 medium eggs, lightly beaten
150 g/5 oz plain flour
175 g/6 oz icing sugar
2 tbsp cocoa powder
15 g/$^1/_2$ oz butter

Food fact

Chocolate is obtained from the bean of the cacao tree and was introduced to Europe in the 16th century. It is available in many different forms, from cocoa powder to couverture, which is the best chocolate to use for cooking, as it has a high cocoa butter content and melts very smoothly.

2

3

5

Celebration Cakes, Cream Cakes & Gateaux

Make a special occasion even more memorable with these recipes for slightly more complex or luxurious cakes that are still simple to make, and indulge in the rich and moist cream cakes and gateaux. From Rich Devil's Food Cake to Wild Strawberry & Rose Petal Jam Cake, you are sure to have your guests delight in your creation.

Fresh Strawberry Sponge Cake

1   Preheat the oven to 190°C/375°F/Gas Mark 5, 10 minutes before baking. Lightly oil and line the bases of two 20.5 cm/ 8 inch round cake tins with greaseproof or baking paper.

2   Using an electric whisk, beat the butter, sugar and vanilla essence until pale and fluffy. Gradually beat in the eggs a little at a time, beating well between each addition.

3   Sift half the flour over the mixture and, using a metal spoon or rubber spatula, gently fold into the mixture. Sift over the remaining flour and fold in until just blended.

4   Divide the mixture between the tins, spreading evenly. Gently smooth the surfaces with the back of a spoon. Bake in the centre of the preheated oven for 20–25 minutes, or until well risen and golden.

5   Remove and leave to cool before turning out on to a wire rack. Whip the cream with 1 tablespoon of the icing sugar until it forms soft peaks. Fold in the chopped strawberries.

6   Spread one cake layer evenly with the mixture and top with the second cake layer, rounded side up.

7   Thickly dust the cake with icing sugar and decorate with the reserved strawberries. Carefully slide on to a serving plate and serve.

Ingredients   SERVES 8–10

175 g/6 oz unsalted butter, softened
175 g/6 oz caster sugar
1 tsp vanilla essence
3 large eggs, beaten
175 g/6 oz self-raising flour
150 ml/¼ pint double cream
2 tbsp icing sugar, sifted
225 g/8 oz fresh strawberries,
    hulled and chopped
few extra strawberries, to decorate

Helpful hint

For sponge cakes, it is important to achieve the correct consistency of the uncooked mixture. Check it after folding in the flour by tapping a spoonful of the mixture on the side of the bowl. If it drops easily, 'dropping' consistency has been reached. If it is too stiff, fold in a tablespoon of cooled boiled water.

Almond Angel Cake with Amaretto Cream

1 Preheat the oven to 180°C/350°F/Gas Mark 4, 10 minutes before baking. Sift together the 175 g/6 oz icing sugar with the flour. Stir to blend, then sift again and reserve.

2 Using an electric whisk, beat the egg whites, cream of tartar, vanilla essence, $1/2$ teaspoon of almond essence and salt on medium speed until soft peaks form. Gradually add the caster sugar, 2 tablespoons at a time, beating well after each addition, until stiff peaks form. Sift about one-third of the flour mixture over the egg white mixture and, using a metal spoon or rubber spatula, gently fold in. Repeat in two more batches. Spoon gently into an ungreased angel food cake tin or 25.5 cm/10 inch tube tin. Bake in the preheated oven until risen and golden on top (about 40 minutes) and the surface springs back quickly when gently pressed with a clean finger. Immediately invert the cake tin and cool completely in the tin. When cool, carefully run a sharp knife around the edge of the tin and the centre ring to loosen the cake from the edge. Using your fingertips, ease the cake from the tin and invert on to a cake plate. Thickly dust the cake with the extra icing sugar.

3 Whip the cream with the remaining almond essence, Amaretto liqueur and a little more icing sugar, until soft peaks form. Fill a piping bag fitted with a star nozzle with half the cream and pipe around the bottom edge of the cake. Decorate the edge with the fresh raspberries and serve the remaining cream separately.

Ingredients
MAKES 10–12 SLICES

175 g/6 oz icing sugar, plus 2–3 tbsp
150 g/5 oz plain flour
350 ml/12 fl oz egg whites
   (about 10 large egg whites)
$1 1/2$ tsp cream of tartar
$1/2$ tsp vanilla essence
1 tsp almond essence
$1/4$ tsp salt
200 g/7 oz caster sugar
175 ml/6 fl oz double cream
2 tablespoons Amaretto liqueur
fresh raspberries, to decorate

Food fact
Angel cake has a very light and delicate texture and can be difficult to slice. For best results, use two forks to gently separate a portion of the cake.

1

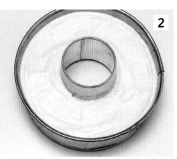
2

3

White Chocolate Cheesecake

1 Preheat the oven to 180°C/350°F/Gas Mark 4, 10 minutes before baking. Lightly oil a 23 x 7.5 cm/9 x 3 inch springform tin. Crush the biscuits and almonds in a food processor to form fine crumbs. Pour in the butter and almond essence and blend. Pour the crumbs into the tin and, using the back of a spoon, press on to the bottom and up the sides to within 1 cm/$^1/_2$ inch of the top. Bake for 5 minutes to set. Remove and transfer to a wire rack. Reduce the oven temperature to 150°C/300°F/Gas Mark 2. Heat the white chocolate and cream in a saucepan over a low heat, stirring constantly, until melted. Remove and cool.

2 Beat the cream cheese and sugar until smooth. Add the eggs, one at a time, beating well after each addition. Slowly beat in the cooled white chocolate cream and the Amaretto and pour into the crust. Place on a baking tray and bake for 45–55 minutes, until the edge of the cake is firm, but the centre is slightly soft. Reduce the temperature if the top begins to brown. Remove to a wire rack and increase the temperature to 200°C/400°F/Gas Mark 6.

3 Beat the soured cream, sugar and almond or vanilla essence until smooth and gently pour over the cheesecake, tilting the tin to distribute evenly. Bake for another 5 minutes. Turn off the oven and leave the door halfway open for about 1 hour. Transfer to a rack and run a sharp knife around the edge of the crust to separate from the tin. Cool and refrigerate until chilled. Remove from the tin, decorate with white chocolate curls and serve.

Ingredients
CUTS INTO 16 SLICES

For the base:
150 g/5 oz digestive biscuits
50 g/2 oz whole almonds, lightly toasted
50 g/2 oz butter, melted
$^1/_2$ tsp almond essence

For the filling:
350 g/12 oz good-quality white chocolate, chopped
125 ml/4 fl oz double cream
700 g/1$^1/_2$ lb cream cheese, softened
50 g/2 oz caster sugar
4 large eggs
2 tbsp Amaretto or almond flavour liqueur

For the topping:
450 ml/$^3/_4$ pint soured cream
50 g/2 oz caster sugar
$^1/_2$ tsp almond or vanilla essence
white chocolate curls, to decorate

1

2

3

Rich Devil's Food Cake

1 Preheat the oven to 180°C/350°F/Gas Mark 4, 10 minutes before baking. Lightly oil and line the bases of three 23 cm/9 inch cake tins with greaseproof paper. Sift the flour, bicarbonate of soda and salt into a bowl. Sift the cocoa powder into another bowl and gradually whisk in a little of the milk to form a paste. Continue whisking in the milk until smooth.

2 Beat the butter, sugar and vanilla essence until light and fluffy then gradually beat in the eggs. Stir in the flour and cocoa mixtures alternately in three or four batches. Divide the mixture evenly among the three tins, smoothing the surfaces evenly. Bake for 25–35 minutes, until cooked and firm to the touch. Remove, cool and turn out on to a wire rack. Discard the lining paper.

3 To make the frosting, put the sugar, salt and chocolate into a heavy-based saucepan and stir in the milk until blended. Add the golden syrup and butter. Bring to the boil over a medium-high heat, stirring to help dissolve the sugar. Boil for 1 minute, stirring constantly. Remove from the heat, stir in the vanilla essence and cool. Whisk until thickened and slightly lighter in colour.

4 Sandwich the three cake layers together with about a third of the frosting, placing the third cake layer with the flat side up. Transfer the cake to a serving plate and, using a metal palette knife, spread the remaining frosting over the top and sides. Swirl the top to create a decorative effect and serve.

Ingredients CUTS INTO 12–16 SLICES

450 g/1 lb plain flour
1 tbsp bicarbonate of soda
$^1/_2$ tsp salt
75 g/3 oz cocoa powder
300 ml/$^1/_2$ pint milk
150 g/5 oz butter, softened
400 g/14 oz soft dark brown sugar
2 tsp vanilla essence
4 large eggs

For the chocolate fudge frosting:

275 g/10 oz caster sugar
$^1/_2$ tsp salt
125 g/4 oz plain dark chocolate, chopped
225 ml/8 fl oz milk
2 tbsp golden syrup
125 g/4 oz butter, diced
2 tsp vanilla essence

Italian Polenta Cake with Mascarpone Cream

1   Preheat the oven to 190°C/375°F/Gas Mark 5, 10 minutes before baking. Butter a 23 cm/9 inch springform tin. Dust lightly with flour.

2   Stir the flour, polenta or cornmeal, baking powder, salt and lemon zest together. Beat the eggs and half the sugar until light and fluffy. Slowly beat in the milk and almond essence. Stir in the raisins or sultanas, then beat in the flour mixture and 50 g/2 oz of the butter.

3   Spoon into the tin and smooth the top evenly. Arrange the pear slices on top in overlapping concentric circles. Melt the remaining butter and brush over the pear slices. Sprinkle with the rest of the sugar. Bake in the oven for about 40 minutes, until puffed and golden and the edges of the pears are lightly caramelised. Transfer to a wire rack. Reserve to cool in the tin for 15 minutes.

4   Remove the cake from the tin. Heat the apricot jam with 1 tablespoon of water and brush over the top of the cake to glaze.

5   Beat the mascarpone cheese with the sugar to taste, the cream and Amaretto or rum until smooth and forming a soft dropping consistency (see page 192's Helpful Hint). When the cake is cool, sprinkle the almonds over the polenta cake and dust generously with the icing sugar. Serve with the liqueur-flavoured mascarpone cream on the side.

Ingredients   CUTS INTO 6–8 SLICES

- 1 tsp butter and flour for the tin
- 100 g/3$^{1}/_{2}$ oz plain flour
- 40 g/1$^{1}/_{2}$ oz polenta or yellow cornmeal
- 1 tsp baking powder
- $^{1}/_{4}$ tsp salt
- grated zest of 1 lemon
- 2 large eggs
- 150 g/5 oz caster sugar
- 5 tbsp milk
- $^{1}/_{2}$ tsp almond essence
- 2 tbsp raisins or sultanas
- 75 g/3 oz unsalted butter, softened
- 2 medium dessert pears, peeled, cored and thinly sliced
- 2 tbsp apricot jam
- 175 g/6 oz mascarpone cheese
- 1–2 tsp sugar
- 50 ml/2 fl oz double cream
- 2 tbsp Amaretto liqueur or rum
- 2–3 tbsp toasted flaked almonds
- icing sugar, to dust

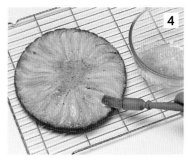

Christmas Cranberry Chocolate Roulade

1 Preheat the oven to 200°C/400°F/Gas Mark 6. Bring the cream to the boil over a medium heat. Remove from the heat and add all of the chocolate, stirring until melted. Stir in the brandy, if using, and strain into a medium bowl. Cool, then refrigerate for 6–8 hours.

2 Lightly oil and line a 39 x 26 cm/15½ x 10½ inch Swiss roll tin with non-stick baking paper. Using an electric whisk, beat the egg yolks until thick and creamy. Slowly beat in the cocoa powder and half the icing sugar and reserve. Whisk the egg whites and cream of tartar into soft peaks. Gradually whisk in the remaining sugar until the mixture is stiff and glossy. Gently fold the yolk mixture into the egg whites with a metal spoon or rubber spatula. Spread evenly into the tin. Bake in the preheated oven for 15 minutes. Remove and invert on to a large sheet of greaseproof paper, dusted with cocoa powder. Cut off the crisp edges of the cake then roll up. Leave on a wire rack until cold.

3 For the filling, heat the cranberry sauce with the brandy, if using, until warm and spreadable. Unroll the cooled cake and spread with the sauce. Allow to cool and set. Carefully spoon the whipped cream over the surface and spread to within 2.5 cm/1 inch of the edges. Re-roll the cake. Transfer to a plate or tray. Allow the ganache to soften at room temperature, then beat until soft and spreadable. Spread over the roulade and mark the roulade with ridges to resemble tree bark. Dust with icing sugar. Decorate with the orange strips and dried cranberries and serve.

Ingredients

CUTS INTO 12–14 SLICES

For the chocolate ganache frosting:
300 ml/½ pint double cream
350 g/12 oz plain dark chocolate, chopped
2 tbsp brandy (optional)

For the roulade:
5 large eggs, separated
3 tbsp cocoa powder, sifted, plus extra for dusting
125 g/4 oz icing sugar, sifted, plus extra for dusting
¼ tsp cream of tartar

For the filling:
175 g/6 oz cranberry sauce
1–2 tbsp brandy (optional)
450 ml/¾ pint double cream, whipped to soft peaks

To decorate:
caramelised orange strips
dried cranberries

Buttery Passion Fruit Madeira Cake

1 Preheat the oven to 180°C/350°F/Gas Mark 4, 10 minutes before baking. Lightly oil and line the base of a 23 x 12.5 cm/9 x 5 inch loaf tin with greaseproof paper. Sift the flour and baking powder into a bowl and reserve.

2 Beat the butter, sugar, orange zest and vanilla essence until light and fluffy, then gradually beat in the eggs, 1 tablespoon at a time, beating well after each addition. If the mixture appears to curdle or separate, beat in a little of the flour mixture. Fold in the flour mixture with the milk until just blended. Do not overmix. Spoon lightly into the prepared tin and smooth the top evenly. Sprinkle lightly with the teaspoon of caster sugar. Bake in the preheated oven for 55 minutes, or until well risen and golden brown. Remove from the oven and leave to cool for 15–20 minutes.

3 Cut the passion fruits in half and scoop out the pulp into a sieve set over a bowl. Press the juice through using a rubber spatula or wooden spoon. Stir in the icing sugar and stir to dissolve, adding a little extra sugar if necessary.

4 Using a skewer, pierce holes all over the cake. Slowly spoon the passion fruit glaze over the cake and allow to seep in. Gently turn the cake out of the tin setting it on to a wire rack the right way up, discarding the lining paper. Dust with icing sugar and cool completely. Serve the Madeira cake cold.

Ingredients
CUTS INTO 8–10 SLICES

210 g/7$\frac{1}{2}$ oz plain flour
1 tsp baking powder
175 g/6 oz unsalted butter, softened
250 g/9 oz caster sugar, plus 1 tsp
grated zest of 1 orange
1 tsp vanilla essence
3 medium eggs, beaten
2 tbsp milk
6 ripe passion fruits
50 g/2 oz icing sugar
icing sugar, to dust

Food fact

Regardless of its name, Madeira cake does not actually originate from the Portuguese-owned island of Madeira. It is, in fact, a traditional English favourite which acquired its name because the cake was often served with the fortified wine, Madeira.

2

3

4

French Chocolate Pecan Torte

1 Preheat the oven to 180°C/350°F/Gas Mark 4, 10 minutes before baking. Lightly butter and line a 20.5 x 5 cm/8 x 2 inch springform tin with non-stick baking paper. Wrap the tin in a large sheet of foil to prevent water seeping in.

2 Melt the chocolate and butter in a saucepan over a low heat and stir until smooth. Remove from the heat and cool.

3 Using an electric whisk, beat the eggs, sugar and vanilla essence until light and foamy. Gradually beat in the melted chocolate, ground nuts and cinnamon, then pour into the prepared tin.

4 Set the foil-wrapped tin in a large roasting tin and pour in enough boiling water to come 2 cm/³/₄ inch up the sides of the tin. Bake in the preheated oven until the edge is set, but the centre is still soft when the tin is gently shaken. Remove from the oven and place on a wire rack to cool.

5 For the glaze, melt all the ingredients over a low heat until melted and smooth, then remove from the heat. Dip each pecan halfway into the glaze and set on a sheet of non-stick baking paper until set. Allow the remaining glaze to thicken slightly. Remove the cake from the tin and invert. Pour the glaze over the cake, smoothing the top and spreading the glaze around the sides. Arrange the glazed pecans around the edge of the torte. Allow to set and serve.

Ingredients

CUTS INTO
16 SLICES

200 g/7 oz plain dark
   chocolate, chopped
150 g/5 oz butter, diced
4 large eggs
100 g/3¹/₂ oz caster sugar
2 tsp vanilla essence
125 g/4 oz pecans, finely ground
2 tsp ground cinnamon
24 pecan halves, lightly toasted,
   to decorate

For the chocolate glaze:

125 g/4 oz plain dark
   chocolate, chopped
60 g/2¹/₂ oz butter, diced
2 tbsp clear honey
¹/₄ tsp ground cinnamon

Food fact

Although this recipe is French, the torte actually originates from Germany, and tends to be a very rich cake-like dessert. It is delicious served with a fruity mixed berry compote.

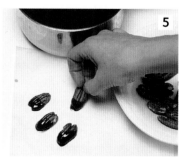

Lemony Coconut Cake

1 Preheat the oven to 180°C/350°F/Gas Mark 4, 10 minutes before baking. Lightly oil and flour two 20.5 cm/8 inch non-stick cake tins.

2 Sift the flour, cornflour, baking powder and salt into a large bowl and add the vegetable fat or margarine, sugar, lemon zest, vanilla essence, eggs and milk. With an electric whisk on a low speed, beat until blended, adding a little extra milk if the mixture is very stiff. Increase the speed to medium and beat for about 2 minutes. Divide the mixture between the tins and smooth the tops. Bake for 20–25 minutes, or until firm and cooked. Remove from the oven and cool before removing from the tins.

3 Put all the ingredients for the frosting, except the coconut, into a heatproof bowl placed over a saucepan of simmering water. Do not allow the base of the bowl to touch the water. Blend on a low speed. Increase the speed to high and beat for 7 minutes, until the whites are stiff and glossy. Remove from the heat and continue beating until cool. Cover with clingfilm.

4 Using a serrated knife, split the cake layers horizontally in half and sprinkle each cut surface with the Malibu or rum. Sandwich them together with the lemon curd and press lightly. Spread the top and sides generously with the frosting, swirling and peaking the top. Sprinkle the coconut over the top and gently press on to the sides. Decorate with the lime zest and serve.

Ingredients CUTS INTO 10–12 SLICES

275 g/10 oz plain flour
2 tbsp cornflour
1 tbsp baking powder
1 tsp salt
150 g/5 oz white vegetable fat
  or soft margarine
275 g/10 oz caster sugar
grated zest of 2 lemons
1 tsp vanilla essence
3 large eggs
150 ml/$^1/_4$ pint milk
4 tbsp Malibu or rum
450 g/1 lb jar lemon curd
lime zest, to decorate

For the frosting:

275 g/10 oz caster sugar
125 ml/4 fl oz water
1 tbsp glucose
$^1/_4$ tsp salt
1 tsp vanilla essence
3 large egg whites
75 g/3 oz shredded coconut

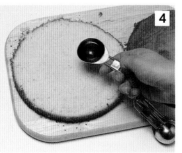

Wild Strawberry & Rose Petal Jam Cake

1 Preheat the oven to 180°C/350°F/Gas Mark 4, 10 minutes before baking. Lightly oil and flour a 20.5 cm/8 inch non-stick cake tin. Sift the flour, baking powder and salt into a bowl and reserve.

2 Beat the butter and sugar until light and fluffy. Beat in the eggs, a little at a time, then stir in the rosewater. Gently fold in the flour mixture and milk with a metal spoon or rubber spatula and mix lightly together.

3 Spoon the cake mixture into the tin, spreading evenly and smoothing the top.

4 Bake in the preheated oven for 25–30 minutes, or until well risen and golden and the centre springs back when pressed with a clean finger. Remove and cool, then remove from the tin.

5 For the filling, whisk the cream, yogurt, 1 tablespoon of rosewater and 1 tablespoon of icing sugar until soft peaks form. Split the cake horizontally in half and sprinkle with the remaining rosewater.

6 Spread the warmed jam on the base of the cake. Top with half the whipped cream mixture, then sprinkle with half the strawberries. Place the remaining cake half on top. Spread with the remaining cream and swirl, if desired. Decorate with the rose petals. Dust the cake lightly with a little icing sugar and serve.

Ingredients   SERVES 8

275 g/10 oz plain flour
1 tsp baking powder
$^1/_4$ tsp salt
150 g/5 oz unsalted butter, softened
200 g/7 oz caster sugar
2 large eggs, beaten
2 tbsp rosewater
125 ml/4 fl oz milk
125 g/4 oz rose petal or strawberry
   jam, slightly warmed
125 g/4 oz wild strawberries, hulled,
   or baby strawberries, chopped
frosted rose petals, to decorate

Rose cream filling:

200 ml/7 fl oz double cream
25 ml/1 fl oz natural Greek yogurt
2 tbsp rosewater
1–2 tbsp icing sugar

Food fact

Rosewater is distilled from rose petals and has an intensely perfumed flavour. It has been popular in the cuisines of the Middle East, China and India for centuries.

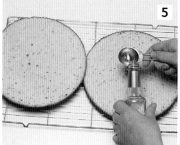

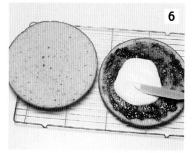

Celebration Fruit Cake

1 Preheat the oven to 170°C/325°F/Gas Mark 3, 10 minutes before baking. Heat the butter and sugar in a saucepan until the sugar has dissolved, stirring frequently.

2 Add the pineapple and juice, dried fruits and peel. Bring to the boil, simmer for 3 minutes, stirring occasionally, then remove from the heat to cool completely.

3 Lightly oil and line the base of a 20.5 x 7.5 cm/8 x 3 inch loose-bottomed cake tin with non-stick baking paper. Sift the flour, bicarbonate of soda, spices and salt into a bowl. Add the boiled fruit mixture to the flour with the eggs and mix. Spoon into the tin and smooth the top. Bake in the preheated oven for 1¼ hours, or until a skewer inserted into the centre comes out clean. If the cake is browning too quickly, cover loosely with foil and reduce the oven temperature. Remove and cool completely before removing from the tin and discarding the lining paper.

4 Arrange the nuts, cherries and prunes or dates in an attractive pattern on top of the cake. Heat the honey and brush over the topping to glaze. Alternatively, toss the nuts and fruits in the warm honey and spread evenly over the top of the cake. Cool completely and store in a cake tin for a day or two before serving to allow the flavours to develop.

Ingredients
CUTS INTO 16 SLICES

125 g/4 oz butter or margarine
125 g/4 oz soft dark brown sugar
380 g can crushed pineapple
150 g/5 oz raisins
150 g/5 oz sultanas
125 g/4 oz crystallised ginger, finely chopped
125 g/4 oz glacé cherries, coarsely chopped
125 g/4 oz mixed cut peel
225 g/8 oz self-raising flour
1 tsp bicarbonate of soda
2 tsp mixed spice
1 tsp ground cinnamon
½ tsp salt
2 large eggs, beaten

For the topping:
100 g/3½ oz pecan or walnut halves, lightly toasted
125 g/4 oz red, green and yellow glacé cherries
100 g/3½ oz small pitted prunes or dates
2 tbsp clear honey

Raspberry & Hazelnut Meringue Cake

1 Preheat the oven to 140°C/275°F/Gas Mark 1. Line two baking sheets with non-stick baking paper and draw a 20.5 cm/8 inch circle on each. Whisk the egg whites and cream of tartar until soft peaks form then gradually beat in the sugar, 2 tablespoons at a time.

2 Beat well after each addition until the whites are stiff and glossy. Using a metal spoon or rubber spatula, gently fold in the ground hazelnuts.

3 Divide the mixture evenly between the two circles and spread neatly. Swirl one of the circles to make a decorative top layer. Bake in the preheated oven for about 1¹/₂ hours, until crisp and dry. Turn off the oven and allow the meringues to cool for 1 hour. Transfer to a wire rack to cool completely. Carefully peel off the papers.

4 For the filling, whip the cream, icing sugar and liqueur, if using, together until soft peaks form. Place the flat round on a serving plate. Spread over most of the cream, reserving some for decorating and arrange the raspberries in concentric circles over the cream.

5 Place the swirly meringue on top of the cream and raspberries, pressing down gently. Pipe the remaining cream on to the meringue and decorate with a few raspberries and serve.

Ingredients

CUTS INTO
8 SLICES

For the meringue:
4 large egg whites
¹/₄ tsp cream of tartar
225 g/8 oz caster sugar
75 g/3 oz hazelnuts, skinned, toasted and finely ground

For the filling:
300 ml/¹/₂ pint double cream
1 tbsp icing sugar
1–2 tbsp raspberry-flavoured liqueur (optional)
350 g/12 oz fresh raspberries

Helpful hint
It is essential when whisking egg whites that the bowl being used is completely clean and dry, as any grease or oil will prevent the egg whites from gaining the volume needed.

Chocolate & Almond Daquoise with Summer Berries

1 Preheat the oven to 140°C/275°F/Gas Mark 1, 10 minutes before baking. Line three baking sheets with non-stick baking paper and draw a 20.5 cm/8 inch round on each one.

2 Whisk the egg whites and cream of tartar until soft peaks form. Gradually beat in the sugar, 2 tablespoons at a time, beating well after each addition, until the whites are stiff and glossy.

3 Beat in the almond essence, then, using a metal spoon or rubber spatula, gently fold in the ground almonds. Divide the mixture evenly between the three circles of baking paper, spreading neatly into the rounds and smoothing the tops evenly. Bake in the preheated oven for about 1¼ hours or until crisp, rotating the baking sheets halfway through cooking. Turn off the oven, allow to cool for about 1 hour, then remove and cool completely before discarding the lining paper.

4 Beat the butter, icing sugar and cocoa powder until smooth and creamy, adding the milk or cream to form a soft consistency. Reserve about a quarter of the berries to decorate. Spread one meringue with a third of the buttercream and top with a third of the remaining berries. Repeat with the other meringue rounds, buttercream and berries. Scatter with the toasted flaked almonds, the reserved berries and sprinkle with icing sugar and serve.

Ingredients

CUTS INTO 8 SERVINGS

For the almond meringues:

6 large egg whites
¼ tsp cream of tartar
275 g/10 oz caster sugar
½ tsp almond essence
50 g/2 oz blanched or flaked almonds, lightly toasted and finely ground

For the chocolate buttercream:

75 g/3 oz butter, softened
450 g/1 lb icing sugar, sifted
50 g/2 oz cocoa powder, sifted
3–4 tbsp milk or single cream
550 g/1¼ lb mixed summer berries such as raspberries, strawberries and blackberries

To decorate:

toasted flaked almonds
icing sugar

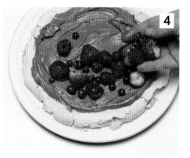

Orange Fruit Cake

1 Preheat the oven to 180°C/350°F/Gas Mark 4, 10 minutes before baking. Lightly oil and line the base of a 25.5 cm/10 inch ring mould tin or deep springform tin with non-stick baking paper.

2 Sift the flour and baking powder into a bowl and stir in the sugar. Make a well in the centre and add the butter, eggs, grated zest and orange juice. Beat until blended and smooth. Turn into the tin and smooth the top. Bake for 35–45 minutes, or until golden and the sides begin to shrink from the edge of the tin. Remove and cool before removing from the tin and discarding the paper.

3 Using a serrated knife, cut the cake horizontally about one third from the top and remove the top layer of the cake. If not using a ring mould tin, scoop out a centre ring of sponge from the top third and the bottom two-thirds of the layer, making a hollow tunnel. Sprinkle the cut sides with the Cointreau.

4 For the filling, whip the cream and yogurt with the vanilla essence, Cointreau and icing sugar until soft peaks form. Chop the orange fruit and fold into the cream. Spoon some of this mixture on to the bottom cake layer, mounding it slightly. Transfer to a serving plate. Cover with the top layer of sponge and spread the remaining cream mixture over the top and sides. Press the chopped nuts into the sides of the cake and decorate the top with the Cape gooseberries, blueberries and raspberries. If liked, dust the top with icing sugar and serve.

Ingredients   CUTS INTO 10–12 SLICES

For the orange cake:
225 g/8 oz self-raising flour
2 tsp baking powder
225 g/8 oz caster sugar
225 g/8 oz butter, softened
4 large eggs
grated zest of 1 orange
2 tbsp orange juice
2–3 tbsp Cointreau
125 g/4 oz chopped nuts
Cape gooseberries, blueberries, raspberries and mint sprigs to decorate
icing sugar, to dust (optional)

For the filling:
450 ml/³/₄ pint double cream
50 ml/2 fl oz Greek yogurt
¹/₂ tsp vanilla essence
2–3 tbsp Cointreau
1 tbsp icing sugar
450 g/1 lb orange fruits, such as mango, peach, nectarine, papaya and yellow plums

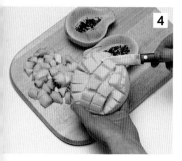

Chocolate Mousse Cake

1 Preheat the oven to 180°C/350°F/Gas Mark 4, 10 minutes before baking. Lightly oil and line the bases of two 20.5 cm/8 inch springform tins with baking paper. Melt the chocolate and butter in a bowl over a saucepan of simmering water. Stir until smooth. Remove from the heat and stir in the brandy. Whisk the egg yolks and the sugar, reserving 2 tablespoons of the sugar, until thick and creamy. Slowly beat in the chocolate mixture until smooth. Whisk the egg whites until soft peaks form, then sprinkle over the remaining sugar and continue whisking until stiff but not dry. Fold a large spoonful of the egg whites into the chocolate mixture. Gently fold in the remaining egg whites. Divide about two thirds of the mixture between the tins, tapping to distribute evenly. Reserve the remaining third of the chocolate mousse mixture for the filling. Bake for about 20 minutes, or until well risen and set. Remove and cool for at least 1 hour. Loosen the edges of the cakes with a knife and lightly press the crusty edges down. Pour the rest of the mousse over one layer, spreading until even. Unclip the side, remove the other cake from the tin and gently invert on to the mousse, bottom side up to make a flat top layer. Discard the paper and chill for 4–6 hours until set.

2 Melt the cream and chocolate with the brandy in a saucepan and stir until smooth. Cool until thickened. Unclip the side of the mousse cake and place on a rack. Pour over half the glaze and spread. Let set, then decorate with curls and the remaining glaze.

Ingredients   SERVES 8–10

For the cake:

450 g/1 lb plain dark
  chocolate, chopped
125 g/4 oz butter, softened
3 tbsp brandy
9 large eggs, separated
150 g/5 oz caster sugar

Chocolate glaze:

225 ml/8 fl oz double cream
225 g/8 oz plain dark
  chocolate, chopped
2 tbsp brandy
1 tbsp each single cream and white
  chocolate curls, to decorate

Food fact

Wonderfully rich and delicious served with a fruity compote – why not try making cherry compote using fresh, if in season, or otherwise tinned in fruit juice? Stone the cherries, or drain, and then simmer on a low heat with a little apple juice until reduced.

Chocolate Box Cake

1　Preheat the oven to 180°C/350°F/Gas Mark 4, 10 minutes before baking. Lightly oil and flour a 20.5 cm/8 inch square cake tin. Sift the flour and baking powder into a large bowl and stir in the sugar. Using an electric whisk, beat in the butter and eggs. Blend the cocoa powder with 1 tablespoon of water, then beat into the creamed mixture. Turn into the tin and bake in the preheated oven for about 25 minutes, or until well risen and cooked. Remove and cool before removing the cake from the tin.

2　To make the chocolate box, break the chocolate into small pieces, place in a heatproof bowl over a saucepan of gently simmering water and leave until soft. Stir it occasionally until melted and smooth. Line a Swiss roll tin with non-stick baking paper then pour in the melted chocolate, tilting the tin to level. Leave until set. Once the chocolate is set, turn out on to a chopping board and carefully strip off the paper. Cut into four strips, the same length as the cooked sponge, using a large sharp knife that has been dipped into hot water. Gently heat the apricot preserve and sieve to remove lumps. Brush over the top and sides of the cake. Carefully place the chocolate strips around the cake sides and press lightly. Leave to set for at least 10 minutes.

3　For the topping, whisk the cream to soft peaks and quickly fold into the melted chocolate with the brandy. Spoon into a pastry bag fitted with a star nozzle and pipe a design of rosettes or shells over the surface. Dust with cocoa powder and serve.

Ingredients　CUTS INTO 16 SLICES

For the chocolate sponge:
175 g/6 oz self-raising flour
1 tsp baking powder
175 g/6 oz caster sugar
175 g/6 oz butter, softened
3 large eggs
25 g/1 oz cocoa powder
150 g/5 oz apricot preserve
cocoa powder, to dust

For the chocolate box:
275 g/10 oz plain dark chocolate

For the chocolate whipped cream topping:
450 ml/³/₄ pint double cream
275 g/10 oz plain dark chocolate, melted
2 tbsp brandy
1 tsp cocoa powder, to decorate

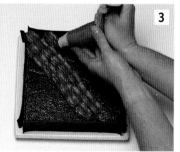

Index